TODAY'S GRANDMOTHER: YOUR GUIDE TO THE FIRST TWO YEARS

A LOT HAS CHANGED SINCE YOU HAD YOUR BABY! THE HOW-TO BOOK TO BECOME AN ACTIVE AND ENGAGED GRANDMOTHER

Angela Bowen, RN PhD

Some photos by Rona Andreas http://www.photopeek.blogspot.ca/

© 2013 Angela Bowen, RN PhD. Facebook: Today's Grandmother "Today's Grandmother?" /
@todays-grandmother

ISBN: 0991939409
ISBN-13: 9780991939404

THIS BOOK IS DEDICATED TO:

*My grandsons, an inspiration and a delight.
My beautiful daughter and her wonderful husband
who brought them into this world.*

*My husband who encouraged me to write this book.
My friends, their children, and grandchildren
who have taught me so much.*

FOREWORD

When we brought home my first newborn son from the hospital, I knew that we were incredibly lucky that my mum was an obstetrical nursing professor. I remember looking to her and asking her "Is this hard enough?" when first burping my son. But, what makes her an excellent grandma is not limited to her nursing experience; she brings to us unconditional love. She lets us all know that her grandsons are the light of her life and she does all she can to support their development, joy, and creativity.

I hope you enjoy this informative, but honest guide to grandparenting and I wish you many laughs and snuggles during this fabulous time in your life.

Lindsay, Angela's daughter.

TABLE OF CONTENTS

CONGRATULATIONS! XIII

1 . GRANDMOTHER. 1
   BENEFITS OF BEING A GRANDMOTHER 1
      For the Child 1 / For the Grandmother 2 / Grandparental Investment 3 /
      Grandmother Hypothesis 4
   MEMORIES 4
      Reliving Your Own Birthing/Parenting Experiences 5 / Were You the Perfect
      Parent? 6
   TRADITIONS. 7
      Keepsakes 8 / What Will You Be Called? 8 / What Is the Baby to be
      Called? 9 / Religion and Culture 10
   ROLE MODEL 11
   WHAT ARE THE NEW PARENTS PLANNING? 12
   RECOGNIZE YOUR LIMITATIONS 14

2. EMOTIONS 17
   HISTORY IS IMPORTANT. 18
   PERINATAL MOOD DISORDERS 19
      Pinks 19 / Baby Blues 20 / Anxiety 20 / Antenatal and Postpartum Depres-
      sion 21 / Postpartum Psychosis 23
   WHAT YOU CAN DO 24
      How to Help 24 / Support 26

TAKING CARE OF YOU...26
The Clubhouse 27 / A Gentler Way to Cope 29 / Positive Mental Health 29

3. RELATIONSHIPS 31
COMMUNICATION...31
What You Say and When You Say It 32 / Are You a Right Fighter? 32 /
Advice 33 / How Not to Alienate the Parents 35 / Parent First 36
HOW TO HELP..37
Babysitting 37 / Their House or Yours 38 / Nannies and Childminders 40 /
Holiday Sitting 40
WHEN A SIBLING COMES ALONG 41
Toddler Regression 41 / How you can help 41
VISITING 42
IN-LAWS...43
Your Son or Son-in-Law 45 / The Other Grandparents 46 / Step-Grand-
mother 47
FINANCIAL SUPPORT 48
Educational plans 49 / Insurance 50

4. PREGNANCY TODAY 51
CONCEPTION...52
Assisted Reproductive Technology (ART) 52 / Gestation 53 / Multiples 54
TESTS 55
Ultrasound 55
PREGNANCY HEALTH...57
Nausea and Vomiting 57 / Vitamins 58 / Folic Acid (Folate) 58 / Weight 59
Normal Weight Gain 60 / Weight issues 61 / Obesity 62 / Infections 62 /
Flu Shot 63
WHEN TO WORRY 64
The Baby 64 / The Mother 66
INFORMATION (OVERLOAD) 66
Prenatal Classes 67 / Online 67 / Social Media 67 /
Health Care Providers 68

5. LABOR AND BIRTHING TODAY............................. 71
PROCESS..71
BEING THERE 73
Home Birth 74 / Water Birth 74 / Induction of Birth 75

WHAT ELSE TO EXPECT. 78
Monitors 79 / Intravenous/Medications 79 / Enemas 80 / Shaving 80 /
Nutrition 80 / Pushing 80 / Vacuum Extraction 81 / Forceps 82 /
Episiotomy and Tears 82 / C-Section 83 / TOLAC/VBAC 83
PAIN RELIEF. 84
Epidural and Spinal Anesthesia/Analgesia 84 / Laughing Gas or Nitrous
Oxide 85 / Other pain relief 85
SOMETHING DIFFERENT 86
Lotus Birth and Eating the Placenta 86

6. TAKING CARE OF MOM. 87
SOME THINGS HAVE CHANGED 87
Conflicting Information from Staff 87
AT HOME. 88
Don't Come Now...Why Aren't You Here? 89
THINGS TO WATCH. 89
Bleeding 89
HOW TO HELP. 90
Housework 90

7. TAKING CARE OF BABY. 93
EARLY CARE 93
Skin to Skin 94 / Bath Time 94
Cord Care 96 / Baby's Eyes and Vitamin K 96
TESTS 97
INFANT NUTRITION 97
How long? 99 / Breastfeeding Support 100 / Bottle, Formula, or
Artificial-Baby-Milk Feeding 101 / Pacifiers 104 / Solids 105 / Readiness
to Eat 106 / Food to Eat 106 / Baby or Infant-Led Weaning 109 / Prepared
Foods 110 / Allergies 110 / Gluten Sensitivity and Celiac Disease 111 /
Beverages 111
COMMON ISSUES 112
Cradle Cap 112 / Colic and Gas 113
Circumcision 115 / Jaundice 116
Teething 117 / Teething Necklaces 118
ELIMINATION—DIAPERS. 118
Diaper Free! 119 / Cloth Diapers 119 / Diapering Systems 120 /
Disposable Diapers 121

Diaper Rash 122 / Baby Powder 124 / Wipes 124 / Potty Training 125

8. BABY HEALTH AND SAFETY TODAY **127**

    HEALTH 127

        Hearing 128 / Vision 128 / Infection 129 / Immunizations 130

    MILESTONES 131

        Shaken Baby Syndrome 133

    SLEEP AND SLEEP SAFETY 133

        Sudden Infant Death Syndrome 133 / "Back to Sleep" 134
        Flathead 135 / Baby and Apnea Monitors 136 / Co-Sleeping and
        Bedsharing 137 / Sleep Sacs 139 / Sleep Training 139 / Crying It Out 140 /
        Cribs and Sleep Surfaces 142 / Tummy Time 143

    HOME SAFETY 144

        Safety Latches 144 / Water Temperature 145 / Pets 146 / Poisons 146

    OTHER SAFETY RISKS 147

        Exposure to Smoke 148 / Sun Safety 149 / Insect Repellent 150

    IS BABY CHOKING OR GAGGING? 151

        The Choking Baby 152 / CPR—Cardio Pulmonary Resuscitation 154

9. EQUIPMENT NOW **157**

    SOMETHING FOR EVERYONE 157

        Car Seats 157 / Strollers 159 / Walkers/Highchairs/Seats 159 / Playpens/
        Play Yards 161 / Gates 162

    THINGS THEY WEAR NOW 162

        Quilts and Blankets 163 / Baby Swaddling 164 / Receiving Blankets 165 /
        Baby Wearing 165 / The Diaper Bag 166 / Clothing 166

    TOYS AND PLAY 167

    AT YOUR HOUSE 169

10. PARENTING TODAY **171**

    ATTACHMENT PARENTING 172

        Attachment Parenting in Practice 173

    BABY SIGN LANGUAGE 174

    BEHAVIOR 175

        Stranger Anxiety and Separation Anxiety 175 / Meltdowns and the Terrible
        Twos 176 / Discipline 176

11. GRANDMOTHER CHALLENGES TODAY 179

GRANDPARENTING FROM A DISTANCE 179

THE SINGLE PARENT AND BOOMERANG CHILDREN 180

DIVORCE AND GRANDPARENT RIGHTS 181

ADOPTION 182

WHEN THINGS DON'T TURN OUT AS PLANNED 183

How to help 184

THE WORST CAN HAPPEN 184

Grief 185 / What about You? 187

WHAT IF YOU AREN'T ENJOYING BEING A GRANDMOTHER? . . . 188

What If You Don't Like Babies? 188 / Not Feeling Appreciated 188

TODAY'S GRANDMOTHER GOES FORTH GENTLY 189

12. TODAY'S RESOURCES 191

PRIVATE OR NON-GOVERNMENTAL ORGANIZATIONS 192

COMMERCIAL SITES 193

GOVERNMENT AGENCIES 194

PROFESSIONAL ORGANIZATIONS 195

BIBLIOGRAPHY 197

ABBREVIATIONS 203

INDEX 205

Congratulations! Your daughter or your child's partner is pregnant. Or, maybe you are becoming a grandmother through surrogacy or adoption. Just when you settled into a predictable life, doing those things you had planned to enjoy once your nest was empty; suddenly your life is set to change again.

As you become a grandparent, your family is now a grandfamily! It is very likely that your relationship with your adult child will evolve and mature. I also hope that you have the pleasure of watching your child become closer to his or her partner as they face the challenges of becoming parents, managing jobs, and making a home and life for their family.

Many of us would like to think we could attract the adoration found in this poem by an anonymous author. One only has to look at the vast assortment of birthday and Mother's Day greeting cards to appreciate the depth of love some hold for their grandmothers.

The most common (and likely the most annoying) comment you will hear about grandchildren is that

What Is a Grandmother?

A grandmother is a remarkable woman.

She's a wonderful combination of warmth and kindness, laughter and love.

She overlooks our faults, encourages our dreams, and praises our every success.

A grandmother has the wisdom of a teacher, the sincerity of a true friend, and the tenderness of a mother.

She's someone we admire, respect, and love very much.

A grandmother will always have a cherished place in our memories and in our hearts.

She's someone for whom we want every happiness in return for the joy she always brings.

A grandmother is all the dear and precious things in life...
When she's a grandmother like you.

http://www.namesandthingszone.com/user/What%20is%20a%20Grandmother.bmp

"you can give them back." It is true—most of us do return them to their parents—but what bothers me the most is the implication of burden. Yes, we are, gulp, older and, sadly, tire more easily, but being a grandmother today can be a sweet and wonderful experience, and many of us have the time and love to give.

While this can be one of the most fulfilling times in your life, it also can be fraught with concern about the health of the mother and safety of the baby and trying to do the right thing for your grandfamily. You may encounter conflicts about differing ways of parenting from your child and his or her partner, but you may also experience tensions around grandparenting with your spouse and, of course, the in-laws!

For most of my forty-year nursing career, I have helped pregnant women give birth and new mothers learn how to care for their new families. I also have taught others to become maternity nurses. I thought I knew a lot about new-baby and mother care, and I was confident about becoming a grandmother. Much to my surprise, it has been a massive learning experience for me. While the physiology of pregnancy and giving birth hasn't changed, somehow having a pregnant person or newborn baby in the family appears to be much more complicated now than it was when we had our children.

If you consider your own experience as the best (and only) way to raise a baby, you could easily find yourself in conflict with your child, aka the new parent.

Our children have many more parenting choices and decisions than we had. They may not be experienced parents (neither were we the first time around), but they are very adept at finding information and communicating with their friends when they aren't sure about things they need to know.

Many expectant and new grandparents have asked me for advice about how to care for their grandchild and avoid problems with the new parents. After reading *Today's Grandmother*, rather than getting frustrated when you think they are doing things wrong or watching their eyes roll back in their heads (yes, they still do this even as adults) when you question their actions, you will know better what to expect.

Understanding something always makes it easier to appreciate those things that are new and unfamiliar to us.

This is a book for women who raised their children in the last thirty years or so or had grandchildren a while ago. So much has changed, since we had our babies. To be helpful, it is essential for grandmothers keep up with the latest in baby and mother care.

I hoped that one day I might become a grandmother, so I have been listening to and watching my friends as they grandparent for a while now. Some things I wanted to emulate, but there were also attitudes and actions I didn't think were successful and I knew I wanted to avoid.

I talked to women about their grandmother experiences—for instance:

- What have you enjoyed the most about being a grandparent?

- What, if anything, scared you the most about becoming a grandparent?

- What is the most important thing for the new grandparent to know or learn?

- What is the biggest change in baby care since you had your children?

I also asked parents who had recently had children for their thoughts about their experiences:

- What was the most helpful thing your baby's grandparents did?

- What did you find to be the most annoying or irritating behavior of your baby's grandparents?

- How did you handle your own feelings when things were not going well with your mother or mother-in-law?

- What information did they give you about childcare that was the complete opposite of what you did with your baby?

I have used quotes from them and explored their responses to give you answers. I have changed their names, but their quotes are real. What is most clear to me is that grandmothers want to do the very best that they can for their grandfamilies and new parents appreciate our help and support in the first two years.

I went to the practice guidelines of obstetricians, pediatricians, and family physicians who care for childbearing families. I also sought out what the numerous government agencies and private groups are saying about very specific conditions such as sudden infant death syndrome. I looked at the books and online resources that many parents are reading these days.

Each of these chapters could be a book itself, I have tried to answer the most important questions, and some resources to learn more if you want to. New research comes out all the time, knowledge evolves, and some guidelines changed while I was writing book. I have done my best to make sure that it accurate and up to date at the time of printing.

Your child and his or her partner may not follow all of the trends in pregnancy and childcare, but there is a good chance you will find this book will help you understand what they are trying to do as new parents. I believe it will help you to avoid conflict with your children and keep your focus on the relationship with your entire grandfamily.

> *I am not a perfect grandmother, mother, or person, but I try to improve myself how and when I can. I continue to learn from the experience of others, science, and my own trial and error.*
>
> *Editing this book at the time of the birth my second grandson, I am reminded of, humbled by, and learn again from my own words*

The most important lessons have come from my grandfamily: my daughter, my grandsons, and my son-in-law. Thankfully, my daughter tells me when I am doing something that isn't quite right or when she does need something, I can help with. I have learned much from my son-in-law, whom I have come to admire and love even more as we have become a grandfamily. The most important teachers are my grandsons, whose needs are immediate, and joys or distastes are instantaneous!

Thank you to Lindsay, Libbye, Rochelle, and Doug for your input, encouragement, and editing.

Recognizing that I am a fortunate grandmother, I will donate a portion of the proceeds from this book to the *Grandmothers to Grandmothers Campaign* of the Stephen Lewis Foundation. This international group provides support to grandmothers in Africa who are raising their grandchildren left orphaned by AIDS (http://www.grandmotherscampaign.org/).

> *Today's Grandmother is a book to help you enjoy and successfully transition into this wonderful new phase of your life.*

Thank you,
Angela Bowen

1. Grandmother

"I am having a grandbaby!" she exclaimed to an acquaintance she had bumped into in the mall. I was sure what I had heard; she was so excited, it was as though she herself was pregnant. As I slowly walked by, they were chatting about the other woman's grandchildren and how lucky she was as she was soon to become a Grandmother!

Benefits of Being a Grandmother

The woman in the mall was right to be pleased, being a grandmother isn't just fun; it also can be very beneficial for your health and that of your grandchildren.

For the Child

Research shows that the more positive attachments a child has, the more likely she, or he is to be socially adjusted. The child feels loved, has someone to confide in (who might not judge

> **A friend summed being a grandmother this way:** *'The most wonderful thing about this experience is my grandbabies—each is different, each is wonderful in his or her own way. The most special part is that I get to spend as much time as I can with them loving them as they are. I do not have to worry about their behavior; they are angels with me. No schedules, no discipline, no worries about their performance. I just get to love them—what a gift!"*
>
> **My daughter read this and said,** *"This is just what drives their sons/daughters nuts!"*

and won't discipline like the parents), and support healthy development. Some have interpreted this benefit of large supports for children as, "It takes a village."

I accept that the more people who love a child, the better; this includes stepparents, aunties, and siblings. At the same time, I believe that the love and connection of a grandparent is special and is to be cherished and nurtured. As a grandmother, you can provide a secure and loving place from which your grandchild can explore the world. Indeed, children thrive on the love of others, and it's up to us as grandmothers to exercise this privilege.

It appears that grandparents, particularly grandmothers, can increase the overall chances of a child's survival. Grandmothers are also influential in the mother's choice to breastfeed, with the grandmother's level of education associated with increase rates of exclusive breastfeeding. Finally, having a grandparent can improve a child's school performance as well as positive behavior and life choices.

For the Grandmother

While there are advantages for the child and family, the biggest benefits may be for us! My husband is a psychiatrist. He encouraged me to write this book when he heard grandmothers-to-be asking me for advice. Mostly, it is because he tells me that his female patients who are depressed often tell him that their greatest source of pleasure in their lives is their grandchildren.

Grandmothering is sometimes the one thing that will get these sad women out of the house; it gives them hope and something to look forward to. It may be that they now have the means to buy their grandchildren presents and take them places that they couldn't have taken their own children when they were growing up. And for some they are hopeful they can have a more positive bond with their grandchildren compared to what they had with their own children, sadly, some having given up on that relationship.

One grandma told me: "I play with my grandkids without worrying about what to cook, when to clean the house, or when to do laundry. I feel that I am truly being in the moment with them."

Providing childcare to grandchildren is linked with greater self-rated health and increased exercise. Let's face it—if you have to keep up with a toddler, it involves some activity, and if you are invited on an outing to the zoo or ice skating, you will be ready for action only if you are fit. Some grandmothers become the primary caretakers for their grandchildren, but that is a unique situation not explored in this book.

Spending time with your grandbabies now helps ensure that when they grow up and become adults, they will feel attached to you. Grandparents who have intense personal relationships with their grandchildren when they are young are more likely to have those children as part of their lives as they age and to receive physical and social support from them.

We aren't old enough to worry about living in a nursing home yet, but I can say from visiting my father in his care home that there are many lonely people sitting in wheelchairs waiting for visitors. Forming enduring relationships with your grandchildren now, while they (and you) are young and healthy, will increase the chances that you are an active part of their life and that you will get visitors thirty years from now.

> One grandmother takes each of her grandchildren on separate lunch dates every month. She catches up with their lives and feels connected to them. This now includes greatgrandchildren.

Two main theories influence today's grandmother: grandparental investment and grandmother hypothesis.

Grandparental Investment

Grandparental investment involves supporting our descendants to ensure that our genetics will survive for more generations. Over the last century, our life expectancy has continued to increase, which leaves more time for grandparenting. While this ought to increase our prospects for experiencing grandparenthood, it hasn't!

Families today are much smaller, and people now delay having children, which

> A friend complained that on Mother's Day her parents ignored her and her sister. *"It's like they love their grandchildren more than us,"* she said.

further decreases our likelihood of becoming a grandparent. This, of course, results in grandchildren who are even more precious to us individually and to society in general.

Our investment (time-related, emotional, and monetary) in our individual grandchildren grows more with each grandchild we have.

Grandmother Hypothesis

The grandmother hypothesis has emerged as we live longer. It suggests that a post-reproductive woman (menopausal and not very likely to have babies) can increase her inclusive fitness (the number of offspring she produces, supports, and adds to the population) by supporting the fertility (conception and giving birth) of her reproductive offspring (her daughters and daughters-in-law) to reproduce (have children).

More simply put, these two theories say that when a grandmother supports her daughter or daughter-in-law in her childbearing and childrearing, she increases those younger women's ability to further conceive and give birth. This improves her grandchildren's chances of surviving and ensures the existence of her family beyond her lifetime, even though she can no longer give birth herself.

MEMORIES

Most of us have memories of being a grandchild. These memories are bound to affect how we parent and how we grandparent. My experience is limited by a lack of grandparents and our move to Canada from the United Kingdom as a child. My maternal grandparents died when my mother was young, from 'consumption' known now as Tuberculosis (TB). There are a few fuzzy pictures of them, but the family was mostly fractured until recently.

As a youngster, I lived a few blocks away from my paternal grandparents. My mother and my grandmother did not get along; I was very aware of this. I was dressed

> If your grandparenting experiences were negative, becoming a grandmother may cause you to reflect on that hurtful time.
>
> *Don't despair; even though you didn't have positive role models, you can read, learn, and do a marvelous job with your own grandfamily.*

up and always told to be on my best behavior around my Grandma, and most importantly to never ask her for anything, lest it show that my mother was not providing for me. Sometimes I would go to church with her. Afterward, we would have tea with cucumber, watercress, and pear sandwiches; it felt very proper and lovely. I saw her only twice after we emigrated when I was eight.

My most positive feelings of a grandparent came from my grandfather. My grandpa was honest and hardworking. He died of lung cancer when I was five and a half years old. Despite the short amount of time he was in my life, he made me feel very special and cherished. I am sure it helped that I was the first girl after five sons and a grandson, but he gave me a feeling of absolute and unconditional love. All children ought to have that feeling, and grandparents are in a unique position to provide it.

If your own parents or in-laws were not active in your children's lives, or if your life as a grandchild was relatively non-existent, like mine, you can make memories for your children and grandchildren to treasure and traditions to share. You can also do as I do and observe and listen to your friends and family who are enjoying the grandparenting relationship:

- What are they doing with their grandchildren and how does it make you feel?

- How do they relate to their children (the new parents)?

- Your siblings or cousins may have had similar experiences as you did with your grandparents, if they have overcome their issues it might help to talk to them.

Reliving Your Own Birthing/Parenting Experiences

I was unprepared for the emotions that emerged and resurfaced with my daughter's pregnancy and with the birth of my first grandchild. Without realizing it, I relived my own disappointing, painful, and traumatic birth, a miscarriage, and the death of my firstborn, fourteen-year-old son.

My daughter and my birth experiences were not what either of us hoped they would be. We were each pregnant while attending university and both of us went overdue. We were both induced, the babies were posterior, and we both needed an emergency Cesarean birth (C-section). We each gave birth to a beautiful baby boy and breastfed him. Both babies became jaundiced.

I thought a lot about how my own mother was absent when my son was born. She lived thousands of miles away and ran her own business. She had chronic bronchitis and often got pneumonia. We did visit them seven weeks after my son was born, but she and my father did not come to visit until he was six months old. My mother-in-law lived a few hundred miles away, but did not ever visit or offer to help. Unfortunately, there was no time-off for fathers beyond the actual birth day in my ex-husband's company then. I am an only child and my friends were all working or busy with their own babies. I was determined that my daughter would feel more supported.

Were You the Perfect Parent?

Be realistic. We are not perfect now, and we weren't then, either. Things happened that no one saw or that you would rather forget, and there are things that you may have blocked out completely!

I kept a journal and a baby book for each of my children for the first few years of their lives. I was very honest with my joys and frustrations. I hadn't looked at these books for almost thirty years. What a revelation to read my own words! Parenting of my children is the highlight of my life, but it was not a perfect time for either my babies or me.

When I reached out to women to learn about their grandmothering experiences, I didn't hear back from a few of them. I tried again. They eventually told me that they could not respond because they did not feel they had done a very good job as either a parent or a grandparent. I was shocked. They have lovely grown children with beautiful children of their own. I truly did not know they felt this way. I had not intended to make them feel badly. I am sure that they, like all of us, did the best they could at the time.

If you weren't satisfied with your parenting, you can try to stop history from repeating itself:

- Be honest with yourself.

— Accept that you did some things very well and other things that you could have done better—you are human.

- Recognize that your child and his or her partner are learning how to become parents.

    — They, just like you, want to do the very best job that they can—in their own way and time.

- Perhaps the best thing you can do to help them is to be patient and to guide and support them as if you were helping them learn to ride a bike.

> There is an important exemption to this: *if what is happening is a life-or-death situation or the parent is completely exhausted and too mentally or physically ill to function properly, then you might have to intervene for everyone's sake. Reserve for emergencies.*

- Try not to step in and save the day and parent for them; resist unless you are asked.

    — Taking over can undermine what may be the fragile esteem of a nervous new parent.

    — There is an important exemption to this: if what is happening is a life-or-death situation or the parent is completely exhausted and too mentally or physically ill to function properly, then you might have to intervene and do what needs to be done for the sake of everyone's health. But, reserve this for times of urgency.

TRADITIONS

When you married, you likely incorporated or adapted your family traditions with those of your partner or started new ones together. And, you likely already had to deal with alterations to those traditions when your child became part of a couple and a new family. Some of this might have included you, or it might not have.

> I recently met a family with a lovely tradition. When a new grandchild is born, they celebrate by bringing the mother's favorite cake with a big "0" candle on top to the hospital and share with the staff.

Becoming a grandfamily today gives you an opportunity to pass meaningful traditions on to your family or to start new traditions as a family.

One friend and her husband felt very left out when her son chose to join his in-laws at a lavish Christmas celebration the first year they were married. Ten years and two grandchildren later, they have yet to be included in this increasingly large family event. It could be a lack of space or it's just how it is done in their family. She has never known the reason for their exclusion, and although she has felt hurt, rather than lament to her son or create family tensions that might do more harm than good, she has said nothing. She, as a very positive person and loving grandmother, accepts this as the reality of her life as an in-law in this family. She and her husband continue to enjoy other celebrations with their son and his family and have found a way to work around it by changing their own traditions on Christmas Day with their other children and grandchildren and making new ones that bring joy.

As a grandmother, you can't do everything, but you have many talents and skills to share with your grandchildren that will be sure to make memories and perhaps will become special traditions associated with you.

Keepsakes

Just as I kept journals of my children growing up, a friend recently gave me a Grandparent's Journal that I will use to make sure I remember these special times with my grandchildren. It would have been nice to have had it from the onset. There are prompts throughout about family events and traditions, and information about family members that you might not think to tell them about now, but that they might cherish later. There are pockets for pictures and cards, and although with digital photos everyone has many photos to look at, you can put your favorites in there and Mother's Day or other cards from your grandchildren. I wish I had something like this from my grandparents or even my parents for my daughter now.

What Will You Be Called?

You are about to get a new title, a new name to indicate your status as a grandmother. There are no limits to the different names that grandparents are called. It might be cultural. I have known many grandmothers called "Baba" (Ukrainian for "grandmother"), "Oma" (Dutch), and "Nana" (used by many western grandmothers, but also those from Kurdistan).

Grandmothers who want to be called "Auntie" don't just appear in the movies. I know of a few women who tried to avoid the "grandmother" label by posing as the baby's aunt rather than her grandmother. I can only assume that this is the ultimate denial about their age. Although the average age of a grandparent is sixty-five, many are in their forties or early fifties, which none of us would consider being remotely old!

I didn't care at all what I was going to be called when I became a grandmother, although I couldn't see myself as "Granny." My daughter is very creative, and I became "Grangela." However, this seemed too hard for my grandson to say, for a while I was "Gammie" now I am Grandma. This suits me just fine.

What Is the Baby to be Called?

Let's face it—unless you have a terminal illness and naming the baby is the parents' last gift to you, it's unlikely that the baby's name is your decision.

One couple I know had to spell their grandchild's name because they couldn't pronounce it. There was no known significance; it was just that the parents liked how the letters looked together! The grandparents struggled with this, but had no choice, and had to learn to say it, although none of us could repeat it.

Having worked in obstetrics for so long, I have seen many unusual names or spellings or simply made up names. Sometimes the initials can spell out odd things;

> A student told me: "When I told my mother what I wanted to name my baby, she was silent. A little while later, she quietly said, 'I don't think I could call a baby by that name.' She was so genuinely upset that I never mentioned it again."

a young man called "Aiden Spencer Smith," for example, may well have difficulty with teasing. Some names, when put together, might take on a new meaning. If the name is one you think the child may be ridiculed for or is somehow offensive, then depending on your relationship with your child, you might try to raise the issue, but otherwise you have to accept it. This might be easier if you can understand why they have chosen such a different name. Is it an in-law family name? Does it have special meaning to them? Is it a popular name right now? Is it on a TV show? On the other hand, the name may have no meaning at all.

If the name is one you think the child may be ridiculed for or is somehow offensive, then depending on your relationship with your child, you might try to raise the issue, but otherwise you have to accept it. This might be easier if you can understand why they have chosen such a different name. Is it an in-law family name? Does it have special meaning to them? Is it a popular name right now? Is it on a TV show?

Religion and Culture

Weddings, births, and death highlight the differences in family values. Hopefully, any contentious religious or cultural issues were resolved during the wedding preparations, if there were any. If the parents aren't married or if your child avoided divisiveness by doing a destination wedding, the birth of a child can highlight conflicts about religious ceremonies or rituals, such as Baptism or Tvilah.

In a famous "All in the Family" episode, Archie Bunker took it upon himself to baptize his grandson, Joey. His son-in-law, "Meathead," was an atheist and did not want any religious celebrations for the baby. Although Archie himself was not overtly religious, he could not stand the thought of his grandson not being baptized, so he arranged to have it done. This was extremely intrusive and it highlights the disrespect that can be inflicted when someone believes so strongly in something that common sense goes out the window.

One mother of three very young children told me that her major issue with her mother-in-law (who lived very close to her) was the difference in their religions. The paternal grandmother was very strict in her beliefs and did not approve of her son not marrying the mother of his children. She spent limited amounts of time with them and would not stay overnight in their home, even when there was a family emergency. The mother said there weren't nasty arguments, but she knew that the grandmother would have been much more engaged and available had they not crossed her religious morals.

Culture can also challenge new parents. It might be difficult to raise a child using the latest guidelines, rather than just following family mores or cultural practices. I think of one family whose parents are immigrants from different countries and whose children were born and educated here. The grandmother asserted her culture during the pregnancy, bringing over special teas or foods for her daughter-in-law to consume. They continued to interfere with the naming of the baby and how they were caring for her. They are a very lovely couple and loyal to their families, but finally the husband had to tell his parents to back off. There were a few weeks of no contact, but things have since resolved, and everyone is talking more openly about all things related to caring for the baby.

ROLE MODEL

While your daughter or son and her or his partner may or not yet be fully grown-up in your eyes, indeed they have produced their own child. Remember that you are still your child's parent and intentional or not, positive or negative, you will continue to be a role model for them.

We have more life experience and if memory serves us, an appreciation for just how challenging it is to become a parent. Sometimes new parents just need an extra set of arms to hold a crying baby while the mother has a long-needed shower or until things calm down. You are modeling patience and giving the new parents a break (and you get to snuggle the baby).

Children will copy everything, and that includes you! One day when my daughter had a cold, my grandson then four months old, tried to copy her coughing. He looked at her closely, and then imitated her perfectly. We were all surprised, but also impressed that he could copy her so well at such a young age. It was a lesson—we had to watch what we were doing and saying in front of him even at that young age.

Some friends and I were talking at dinner one night, and the more experienced grandparents there reminded us to be careful what you do or say because even young

We don't ever want to teach children to keep "secrets" from their parents.

11

grandchildren will tell their parents if you are doing something that perhaps the parents don't wish you to do. However, children telling their parents what is going on in their lives is a good thing that we do not ever want to discourage.

For a child's safety,

- Never ask a child to keep a secret or tell her that she cannot be honest with her parents about things she is doing with you or anyone else.

  — This might make them more vulnerable to abuse or bullying.

- Perhaps wait until the child is old enough to know not to tell mommy if you help the child buy her a birthday gift or plan a surprise rather than telling her not to tell her parents about something that is happening with her.

- Doing things that the child knows she shouldn't do so you can have fun with her, can come back to bite you.

  — A young child is very likely to tell her parents the fun she had and then you really will be in trouble with the parents.

WHAT ARE THE NEW PARENTS PLANNING?

If your daughter or daughter-in-law has a partner, it is unlikely that you can attend prenatal classes with her, but there are other ways to be involved and learn about what is going on. It is essential to know how they plan to parent so that you understand what they are doing, but also so that you do not cause problems for or with them:

- Listen to what they are saying to each other about becoming parents.

- Listen to what they are saying about the habits of other new parents they know.

  — While they may appear overly idealistic to you about their future parenting styles and skills (as we all were back then), how they talk about the parenting of others (disgusted or enthusiastic) might be a clue of what they plan to do or avoid, so listen carefully.

- Listen, listen, and listen.

Read the books they are reading or follow the websites they frequent. It will help to prepare you for what is to come. I cannot say it often enough—so many things have changed, and you need to update yourself. Be careful how you do it.

> Learn along with your son or daughter to know what they expect about childbirth and babycare.

The Internet is full of information, but sometimes it can be confusing, erroneous, and even potentially malicious. This includes blogs written by parents who think their way is best, those selling various services and items, and all kinds of other "experts" who will advise your child as she or he becomes a parent.

We had limited sources of information; my Dr. Spock book became as dog-eared as my *Joy of Cooking*! Today Dr. Sears and Dr. Karp appear to have replaced Dr. Spock. They are popular with many parents right now. I am not endorsing them; I am just letting you know what your children may be reading.

- *The Baby Book: Everything You Need to Know About Your Baby from Birth to Age Two*

  — This is a tome of a book written by the Sears' family of doctors and nurses, parents, and grandparents.

  — It is very pro-attachment parenting and critical of letting babies cry.

  — Some parents may find it hard to follow all their edicts, but they do cover many helpful topics.

- *Happiest Baby on the Block* (There is also a version about toddlers.)

  — This is a very easy-to-read book. I agree with Dr. Karp's five S's for baby care (shown below). I remember using many of his tips, and likely, you will too!

    1. Swaddling

2. [Supervised] Side/stomach position (but not for sleep)

3. Shushing sounds

4. Swinging

5. Sucking (pacifiers)

Be open to and perhaps try to initiate discussions about what they are reading or what you see online. By asking the new parents, you will show your readiness and intention to do things their way. It will also:

- Flatten out any advantage that you thought your parenting experience gave you!

- Set the stage to help your child become a confident, knowledgeable parent who can come to you to discuss baby care and ask for your opinion rather than avoiding you or your input.

- Show them you are serious about following their lead as the parents.

RECOGNIZE YOUR LIMITATIONS

Let's face it, we are all getting on, and some of our bodies have gone through the mill and back. Many of us take anti-arthritis or hypertension medications. Some of us may have always had limitations, for instance:

Physical: My knee has been a problem my entire life. I had numerous surgeries before I had a total knee replacement in my forties. I wasn't able to run or ice skate as a child or with my own children. I am presently awaiting shoulder surgery.

I will be a grandma who pushes a stroller or reads (and reads and reads.... Last night I read at least twenty books to my grandson). Those things I will be able to do for a long time to come as well as draw, paint, playdough, cooking, cars and blocks. We have a raised sandbox, and I sit on a chair while we happily play.

Vision: I would imagine the very best of hugs come from a blind grandma wanting to absorb everything about her grandchild.

One wonderful grandmother story is about ten-year-old Dylan Viale from California. His grandmother had been blind since well before he was born. He developed a video game for his school science project to direct play on the game by sound rather than sight so that his grandmother could play with him. True love.

Hearing: Until a friend shared her fears about her recent hearing loss, I had not realized the extent of concern it might cause for grandparents. She uses very good hearing aids, but she is still fearful of not being able to hear her grandchildren while she is sleeping or when turned away from them. Her grandchildren have learned to communicate with her differently than they do with other people, but it does worry her.

Be honest about your limitations:

- Does your health affect how you might be able to respond in an emergency?

- Do your children know of all of your limitations? Medications you may be taking?

- Can you attend or take your grandchildren to swimming class or other activities?

- Do you do any crafts they might enjoy doing with you and that you can teach them?

> The best thing you can do is to determine what you can do and then do it as well and as often as possible.

2. EMOTIONS

Pregnancy and childbirth can be an emotional time for the entire family. I walked into my house the first time after the birth of my son and burst into tears. We had just moved the day before I went to the hospital to have him. Nothing had changed in the seven days I was gone—no curtains had magically appeared on the windows, there were unopened boxes everywhere, and just a bassinette and bed were ready. The first time I took a shower in my 'new' house, water leaked all over the bathroom into the hall. I cried again.

I also realized that I was home with a new baby. This baby was not in the hospital anymore, where, as a nurse, I felt competent and had many friends around me; instead, I was a tired, sore, new mother vulnerable to the needs of my own baby! I was fortunate that I had a very calm and easy baby, and soon my confidence and physical health improved. I slowly unpacked and settled into my new life, I now remember it as one of the most cherished times of my life.

My daughter also burst into tears as her husband drove their new baby and us home from the hospital. I was concerned, but she quickly assured me that hers were

> The emotional roller coaster that many women experience in pregnancy or during the postpartum period can accentuate potential misunderstandings, and cause harm to relationships that may never be fully repaired.

tears of joy about being out of the hospital and going home to her own bed and comforts.

Women who are pregnant or postpartum do tend to be more emotional and hypersensitive than at other times in their life. It is also very important for you to realize that you may be perimenopausal or menopausal right now, and you could be experiencing your own renaissance of hormonal emotionality and mood instability!

HISTORY IS IMPORTANT

This is a time for you to think about your previous interactions with your daughter (-in-law) or stepdaughter (-in-law). Your experience with her in stressful or excitable situations will most likely recur during pregnancy and the postpartum period.

If your daughter is the one who is pregnant, you have an obvious advantage. You have had a lifetime of learning each other's idiosyncrasies. You know how she handles stress, hormonal shifts, and your "helpful" suggestions about her decisions. If you have a relationship that has been very volatile, especially during her hormonally charged teenage years, you might expect more of the same, or if you are lucky, she may have mellowed as she matured.

Think back:

- Was she independent from a very young age?

- Did she have PMS, or is she moody and hypersensitive?

- Did you fight often and make up quickly, or were there long periods of silence?

- Does she confide in you and come to you for advice, or does she go to someone else or does she solve problems herself?

Every relationship is different, but if you have had difficult times with your daughter, you may need to be more cautious with her now.

- Please be kind to the new parents and yourself during such interactions.

— You are all likely very tired and more prone to be emotionally overwhelmed and hypersensitive than usual.

> *My advice to you is to be easy with your advice to them.*

— Think of how you would have felt when you had your first baby if someone had said what you are thinking of saying.

- You may have done everything you can think of doing, including being available and settling the baby, and sometimes still be on the receiving end of emotional turmoil and outbursts.

- You don't have to accept rudeness, but realize that sometimes, some things are best ignored.

Emotions, exhaustion, sleep deprivation, hormones, establishing breastfeeding, perhaps with a fussy baby, and the physical recovery from a difficult delivery all can lead to a trying time for new parents.

Be aware that around 20 percent of pregnant and postpartum women experience mental health problems, such as anxiety and depression. And, many women have pre-existing mental health problems that are aggravated during motherhood. The World Health Organization (WHO) identifies depression as the number one cause of disease burden in childbearing women worldwide.

PERINATAL MOOD DISORDERS

If you had anxiety or depression while pregnant or after your baby was born, you know how difficult it can be. But, if you have never had anxiety or depression, you may not realize the empty, confusing, devastating, hopeless, or guilt-ridden feelings a new mother can have. Many women do not share how they are feeling, so you need to be aware of symptoms that might indicate what is going on.

Pinks

The pinks are elation that mothers experience shortly after birth. We expect that new parents will be happy, but for women with a history of bipolar depression or for those with sleep problems, this euphoria can be a worrisome situation that puts them at risk for developing severe depression or psychosis later.

Baby Blues

Most people have heard about the "baby blues," which affect about 80 percent of women. Like me, you likely experienced them, too:

- The blues includes teariness, irritability, and sadness in the first few weeks postpartum.

- Severe blues can be a risk for postpartum depression, so don't ignore the symptoms if you think things are getting worse or not easing up.

- If you notice that the new mother isn't feeling happier after a few weeks, you need to discuss it with her and her partner.

Anxiety

Anxiety is a common mood disorder, affecting around a quarter of pregnant women. Women who experience anxiety during pregnancy are three times more likely to be depressed postpartum. Identifying and treating anxiety early may prevent future depression.

Symptoms of anxiety include a constant sensation of worry or tension, even when there is little or no reason. Here is a partial list of symptoms:

- Excessive worry about the baby and her health, the pregnancy, family or relationship problems, work issues, money, the new parents' health

- Problems concentrating

- Fatigue

- Irritability

- Difficulty falling or staying asleep
  - Sleep that is restless and not refreshing

- Restlessness
  - Startling very easily

Pregnant and postpartum women are at increased risk of developing or worsening anxiety disorders such as panic, OCD (obsessive compulsive disorder), PTSD (post-traumatic stress disorder), and social anxiety.

Women with severe anxiety can lack interest in their baby, fear being alone with the baby, be over intrusive with the baby, or worry about over-attending to the baby. Some constantly check and disrupt the baby, causing irritability, which furthers the problem as they worry about what is wrong.

Antenatal and Postpartum Depression

Most people have heard of postpartum depression (PPD), but antenatal depression or depression during pregnancy is a new concept for many. You need to know the following:

- A history of depression in the woman or her family put her at higher risk for depression.

- Women are likely to have more anxiety symptoms in pregnancy and more depression symptoms after the baby is born.

- Anxiety and depression are treatable, but a mother may resist being identified with a problem and may not agree to being assessed or treated.

- If you are concerned about your daughter or daughter-in-law, talk to her about what you see and why you are worried.

- If you believe she is depressed, you may also want to talk to her partner.

This can all be very stressful for everyone.

> *If you think there might be a problem and your relationship is strained, talk to someone you both trust.*

If a woman experiences five or more of the following symptoms during a two-week period for most of the day, and includes the first and/or second symptom below, she may be depressed:

1. Depressed mood

2. Diminished interest or pleasure in all or most activities

3. Significant weight loss when not dieting, weight gain, or decrease or increase in appetite

4. Insomnia or hypersomnia

5. Excessive or lowered physical expression/activity

6. Fatigue or loss of energy

7. Feelings of worthlessness or excessive or inappropriate guilt

8. Diminished ability to think or concentrate, or indecisiveness

9. Recurrent thoughts of death, recurrent suicidal ideation, or suicide attempt.

Other symptoms often seen, but not included in the above list include irritability, intrusive thoughts, and an inability to cope.

A symptom of depression unique to new mothers can be a preoccupation with the baby's health, which can range from over concern to delusions. It can involve either not attending to baby at all or not letting anyone else care for the baby. Some researchers have recently described "intense parenting" where parents' lives revolve around their children. It is associated with mothers who are depressed.

> Many care providers screen pregnant and postpartum women with the Edinburgh Postnatal Depression Scale. It can be accessed online at www.fresno.ucsf.edu/pediatrics/downloads/edinburghscale.pdf.
>
> *A score of 12 or more can signal depression. Any indication of harm to her or others needs to be investigated. I don't advise you to give it to the woman, but if she is screened, you will know what and why it is happening.*

These mothers believe that:

- The mother, not the father, is the most essential and capable parent.

- Parents' happiness is derived primarily from their children.

- Parents must always provide their children with stimulating activities that help their development.

- Parenting is more difficult than working.

- A parent must sacrifice her needs for the needs of the child.

Postpartum Psychosis

Psychosis is a very serious psychiatric problem that includes agitation, hallucinations, severe mood swings, loss of reality, and/or bizarre perceptions. Untreated, it can lead to suicidal or homicidal thoughts and actions.

- It is very rare for a pregnant woman to become psychotic or to commit suicide, but once the baby is born, postpartum psychosis affects one to two women per thousand births.

- It commonly occurs within the first few weeks after the baby is born, but also can occur months later.

One woman wept as she described her lovely young daughter-in-law, "She was like a ghost, wandering around the house. We all looked after the baby; she wouldn't even look at her. It took months of treatment, but now she is herself again." There is another baby due soon and the mother is being monitored closely by her psychiatrist.

- Women with severe untreated depression who have a bipolar disorder, have mood problems, or are severely sleep-deprived are at an increased risk to experience psychosis.

WHAT YOU CAN DO

When I interviewed women who had attended a local postpartum depression support program, many told me that if their mother or mother-in-law had not experienced depression themselves, they found them to be mostly unsympathetic and judgmental. This caused them to close them out of their lives at a time when they most needed help. Instead of offering support, their well-meaning mothers and mothers-in-law would tell the suffering woman to be happy and thankful that they had a healthy baby, nice house, attentive husband, and to go for a walk.

While going for a walk is healthful for mother and baby, telling a new mother to be thankful for things in her life will not prevent or alleviate depressive symptoms; rather, it is more likely to alienate her. You may be told to leave, which might mean that she is then alone and depressed with her new baby. Not a good scenario.

How to Help

You can help by becoming aware of the symptoms of anxiety and depression. You might ask her gently if she is feeling sad, though she might not always recognize that she is sad or depressed.

> Perhaps the new mother is sleep deprived and still recovering physically; ask what you can do to help. She may just need you to take the baby while she rests, do some chores, and offer behind the scenes support.
>
> *But if this doesn't help, if she is increasingly withdrawn and not responding to anyone, including the baby, avoiding eye contact, or just saying in monotone voice, "I'm fine," and looking unwell, you need to stay close by. If things get worse, more vigilance and action might be required.*

If you are concerned about the safety of the mother or baby, do the following:

- Call her partner (and yours).

- Do not leave her alone. If she banishes you from the house, stay close by.

- Take her to her doctor or to an emergency department to be assessed.

- If she will not go, call a hotline or crisis line and ask her to talk with them.

- If you are on the phone with her, keep her on the line and use another phone to call her partner or a crisis service.

She may be angry with you at the time, but you need to know you have done everything to keep their family safe, and she will eventually know that you have done it because you love them.

Research has shown that babies of women who are depressed are more likely to have health, feeding, and sleeping problems. If the mother is untreated, the children have more emotional, learning, and behavioral problems and developmental delays as they grow. These problems can be partially offset by a healthy partner or significant others (like you) in the baby's life, but having a mentally healthy mother is vital to the growing child.

In addition to the effects on the child, it is not easy living with or being around someone who is depressed. Combined with a lack of sleep and carrying the load of caring for baby and mother, this can take its toll on everyone, especially the new father. It is important to note:

- If a woman is depressed, her partner is fifty percent more likely to be depressed, too, and the chances are even greater if she is severely depressed.

- Fathers tend to become depressed later than the mother does.

- The symptoms of depression are the same for men as for women, but men may be more angry or withdrawn or may turn to alcohol or drugs.

> *If the mother is depressed, it can affect everyone around her.*
>
> *Keep an eye on the new father for signs of exhaustion, depression, or substance use.*

Support

Mental health problems can be treated with various medications and professional therapies. Medications can be controversial, but medical organizations agree that it is better to treat a pregnant woman or new mother who is depressed. An important protective factor against postpartum depression is support. Family, including her partner and you, can provide emotional and physical support with baby and house care, but many women find support groups very helpful. Postpartum Support International (PSI- http://www.postpartum.net/) is an excellent site for everyone.

TAKING CARE OF YOU

Much of *Today's Grandmother* is about giving what you can give and understanding the new grandfamily. If you have a history of depression or if you are burning the proverbial candle at both ends, helping with your new or older grandchild, working, perhaps doing housework at two houses, or not getting enough sleep, you could feel exhausted, and your mood might be low as well.

> There is a very good reason why women our age rarely have babies.
>
> Most of us wear out sooner than when we were younger, so we need our rest.

I tried to help my new grandfamily as best I could, being there whenever my son-in-law wasn't for the first while. One Saturday morning, I got up and had breakfast. I was so tired that I quietly went back to bed. My husband assumed I had gone to my daughter's house as I had on other days. He was very surprised when I walked out of the bedroom at 2:30 p.m. in my nightgown. I hadn't done that since I worked night shifts!

> Realize, you can only do so much, and when people are used to you doing everything for everyone, it is sometimes never enough.

More than one grandmother told me about feeling drained—not just physically tired, but emotionally exhausted by doing so much as a new grandparent and at the same time sometimes being made to feel that all she did just wasn't enough or by feeling that she was intruding and "walking on eggshells" with the new parents.

One woman I know travelled a few thousand miles away to help her daughter, each time she had a baby. The births were normal and she thought everyone adapted well. Despite having other children and grandchildren, a job, and a frail mother, the daughter was angry and dismissive with her for not doing more than with her last baby. She told me she was stunned and hurt; she had tried her best. It might be helpful to spell out how much you can help and keep expectations realistic.

> One wise young mother summarized it this way: *"I have a lot of mommy friends who have struggled with the grandparent relationship. A lot of that is due to expectations that they are going to want to drop everything to look after the baby or that they are going to be a huge help... but then if they aren't, then disappointment and sometimes a negative relationship arises."*

The Clubhouse

The phrase "sandwich generation" describes families who care for three generations: their parents, themselves, and their own children. Now a woman can find herself to be in a "clubhouse" situation (I thought I invented this term until I went online).

The clubhouse involves providing direct care for or feeling responsible for four or five generations. In addition to her immediate family (her husband and herself), the clubhouse woman may have aging parents and perhaps in-laws (which can include stepparents), elderly aunts and uncles, all of whom can have health problems and transportation needs, as well as their own grandparents with multiple needs. Add to this, trying to support and help adult children and grandchildren, and you can see how it is very easy for a superwoman to emerge and then sadly to burn out.

> A calm grandma told me: *"Just as you would likely tell your daughter or daughter-in-law that she doesn't have to be a superwoman, you don't have to be a supergrandwoman."*

Being part of such a family can provide a marvelous community of love, but it also can overwhelm the grandmother who may still be working or have other social responsibilities.

For example, one woman I know has four children and five grandchildren in different cities. Her elderly, widowed mother and mother-in-law live in another city, and her husband has a demanding job that requires him to travel. One of her children has a serious health issue that required many medical visits. She retired early, so everyone imagined she was available to help each of them with their individual needs. As you can imagine, this is a truly exhausting situation for anyone to cope with. She has had to say "no" a few times to various trips to feel that she has equally cared for them all, but the family has not always appreciated her need to take care of herself or the other members who also want her to help them.

It's hard when you are caught up in a demanding situation, but try to protect yourself:

- Be aware of burn out.
  - Exhaustion, cynicism about your role within the family, resentment about what you are doing, and becoming increasingly ineffective in all you do can mean you are burning out.

- Seek balance. Avoiding burnout is all about balance between what you perceived to be work and pleasure in life.
  - Be an active grandparent who is energized and helpful, but also one who knows the boundaries between being involved and taking over (unless in an emergency).

- Continue (or start) some exercise.
  - You need to be in shape so that you can keep up when the baby becomes a toddler and the next one comes along!
  - This can include pushing a grandchild in a stroller or baby aquasize. Do not feel guilty or let anyone try to make you feel guilty about doing something just for yourself like Pilates or dinner with your husband.

> Someone I thought to be very fit told me, *"The one thing I would do differently as a grandmother is to get in shape before the baby is born. I wish I had gone for more walks with my daughter-in-law and to the gym more often. Being a grandmother is a lot of fun, but it's exhausting"!*

- Divide your time wisely to meet your own needs and those of your partner, your grandfamily, your other children, adult parents, and anyone else who is important in your life.

A Gentler Way to Cope

Through the practice of mindfulness and staying in the present moment, we can try to maintain calm awareness and avoid unnecessary negativity. The full practice of mindfulness involves different concepts and tenets of the Buddha.

One simple thing that may help you get through some rough times is controlled breathing and saying affirming statements to yourself. I have heard many different versions, but you can go for a walk or to a quiet place in the house and try saying to yourself, "Breathing in I let go of anger. Breathing out I feel love" or "Breathing in I let go of pain. Breathing out I feel good." Do this or anything comforting to you a few times, using any calming, loving phrase that makes sense to you, and I guarantee you will feel better.

Positive Mental Health

You can help promote the overall mental health of others in your life, depressed or not. One effective way is through affirmations. Affirmations are simply things that you can say that focus on a person's strengths.

You can use simple statements such as "Look at how the baby looks at you; she knows you are her mommy" or "Your mommy takes such good care of you" to the baby or "You look marvelous" to the pregnant woman (but do not say it if she looks bad or you know that she feels terrible!). Honest affirmations can promote feelings of self-esteem and confidence as well as support the new parents during times of change and doubt.

> Say something positive to someone you love; you will both feel better.

I try to convey affirmations on my daughter and other new mothers I know, and I must admit it is a treat to have my daughter affirm my role as her sons' grandmother. It makes me feel warm and appreciated.

I gave a friend a copy of this book whilst it was in its early stages. She and her daughter have had some rocky times, like most mother/daughter relationships. She wanted this to be a good experience for them. She did so many things right; she anticipated some emotional reactions, let them ride by, and bolstered the new parents' self-esteem. She has committed to spend regular time with her new grandfamily—with a concrete plan, everyone will know what to expect and she can stay close without burning out or feeling guilty. I know they will continue to flourish as a new family. She sent me this email:

"Ashley was emotional a couple days after baby was born - her doctor had told her to expect it and so did I as she tends to be emotional - gets that from her mum!! She broke down in tears and told me that she was not experiencing the baby blues, but was feeling really badly, because she knew that she had not treated me well, and said some hurtful things, and I had been so nice. So I gave her big hugs and told her not to make herself feel guilty, all has been forgiven and forgotten (which is true - I can't remember what hurtful things she said - I am really blessed that I don't hold onto things!). So the 2 weeks were a wonderful bonding experience for us, of course there were more tears when I left, but I told her she and Troy will be just fine, and they will be great parents."

What a wise friend I have and what a wonderful grandma she will be!

If reading this section has triggered any uncomfortable feelings for you speak to someone about them or if you have any symptoms of anxiety or depression, please talk to your doctor.

3. Relationships

Even if she is not depressed, communication with the mother-to-be or new mother can be laden with potential triggers for misunderstanding. Sadly, I know of too many grandparents who are not in contact with or have limited access to their grandchildren, sometimes because they said or did something that alienated their grandchild's parents. Good communication is crucial. You can teach a lot by apologizing and not holding resentments over things that are trivial or not intentionally hurtful.

Communication

Whether it is your daughter (who knows that you will always love her) or your daughter-in-law (who may still be uncertain about the relationship), there may be times when she is exhausted or stressed and she lashes out at you. If your relationship is already strained, and she is very angry, she may ignore or shut you out of their lives for a period. Verbal outbursts can be very hurtful. Try not to react.

The relationship with your daughter or daughter-in-law isn't all up to you, but following some of the suggestions here and trying to gain understanding into your own behaviour will help you become and remain engaged in their lives.

You do not want to generate an explosion with what you assume to be well-meaning suggestions, intentions, or actions that may be interpreted as being bossy.

What You Say and When You Say It

There is something about the birth of a new baby that drives people—

> Sometimes the things that need to change are your ideas and how you express them.

women in particular—to want to tell their own parenting stories and to give much uninvited advice about pregnancy and baby care. For some people, telling others what to do is an uncontrollable compulsion!

I know of one family whose members are no longer on speaking terms because of some unsolicited, poorly delivered advice about infant feeding. This situation could have been avoided, or at least could have been less disastrous, if these grandparents had been up-to-date in baby care. They could have asked the parents why they were doing certain things if they were worried, or they could have done some research online, spoken to health professionals before accusing the parents of doing harm when they were following the latest guidelines for feeding their baby. By being uninformed, they were hurtful.

This is also a prime example of the most frequent unsolicited comment from my grandparent friends and the young mothers I know: *Do not give advice unless asked*. This might be a good time to reflect on the Serenity Prayer.

I know that as parents, we have all experienced and survived many different experiences, and as always, we want to help our children avoid our mistakes, discomforts, or disappointments whenever possible. This is true no matter what the issue is

> **The Serenity Prayer**
> *God, grant me the serenity to accept the things I cannot change, the courage to change the things I can, and the wisdom to know the difference.*

and how old our children are. We have to let them find their way.

Are You a Right Fighter?

My daughter introduced me to this term: "Right fighter." Dr. Phil popularized it, and I like it. I know of many people who are right fighters. I know

> The goal is to nurture and preserve the relationship, not to win the battle.

that I was one, especially when safety was involved—or heck, sometimes I know I am right. Overall, my energies in this area have diminished with age and wisdom!

"Right fighting" is an interesting concept worthy of your consideration because I really do think that a right-fighter grandmother would be a lousy grandparent and risk alienating the new parents, particularly her daughter-in-law. It might be OK in a crisis to be right and fight to the death, but I do not think it is what we want to teach our children. The right-fighter grandmother is headed for trouble with her children (unless she has already verbally beaten them into submission), her in-laws, and most importantly, her grandchildren, as they get older!

Ask yourself, and be honest, are you a right fighter?

- Do people ask you why you always have to be right?

- Do you fight to prove your point (which is always right)?

- Do your arguments typically end with you having the last word, but nobody (including you) feeling good about what has happened?

If you see yourself here, you might want to think about the importance of being loved, appreciated, and respected rather than being "right." Ask yourself:

> One very calm grandma to eight wrote, "You are not in competition with your child about who is the best parent; your job is to support them to be the parent they want to be."

- "Is your grandchild's bedtime routine or how long she is breastfed really worth risking the whole relationship over?"

- "Do you want your grandchildren to continue the legacy of right fighting?"

Advice

You can expect that your child will seek out your advice on certain things, but other times, they will want to experience it all themselves and come to their own conclusions, and why not? They are adults whom you have raised to be intelligent, thoughtful, and balanced.

Still, I know that one of the hardest things to do, as a parent, is to believe that you know the possible negative outcome of a situation and to remain silent. You can feel like bursting. At times like this, it is good to have a supportive partner or close friend to whom you can vent your frustrations. Better yet, let go completely and realize that if you are the parent you think you are, you have raised a fine young person who can make good decisions.

This is not to say your children won't want to hear about some of your parenting stories. They will likely enjoy hearing how much the baby looks and behaves like them as a baby. If they ask for your advice, then

> Hearing about our all our struggles and accomplishments doesn't help the new parent who is feeling overwhelmed.
>
> As one mother of two told me, *"If we put our kids on their bellies to sleep as our mothers did, maybe we'd get more sleep, be less stressed, and get more work done too!"*
>
> Some babies do sleep well on their tummies rather than their backs, but it puts them at increased risk of dying from SIDS (See–SIDS). A risk we didn't know about thirty years ago.

of course it is fine to give it, but think about the effects of what you might be saying. If it is something that you found easy and you know that they are struggling with it (such as breastfeeding), you might want to temper your enthusiastic response.

Like most of the women I know, there was little, help from grandparents or relatives with the birth or raising of my children, no microwave or dishwasher, my husband worked very long hours, and yet I canned their baby food, knit their sweaters, and made quilts. Perhaps I was just too exhausted to remember what really happened. Other grandmothers tell me that they also don't know how they did what they did at the time, now that they see how much work it is for their children to raise their grandchildren.

Your child may be interested in your own parenting follies, of which there were likely many. One I have told many parents over the years still mortifies me. We teach parents to clip a baby's nails with nail clippers rather than scissors or biting them off. When I tried to use big nail clippers with my firstborn, I accidentally cut a small tip off his finger. Horrified, I was able to stop the bleeding, but I felt sick and cried about what I had done. I tell parents about this not only to let them know how tricky it can be to cut a baby's very soft but sharp fingernails and to encourage them to get ba-by-sized nail clippers, but also to let them know that we all make mistakes, and accidents do happen.

How Not to Alienate the Parents

There may be times when you are truly concerned for the baby's or the mother's safety or health. You have to approach these concerns with tact and diplomacy. I am not sure that there is a perfect way to raise things you are worried about, and perhaps even this question would be risky if said to some parents:

- Say, "When do babies eat solids now?" rather than saying what you might be thinking, "I gave you cereal at three months, and you survived."

Other things you can do to safeguard the relationship:

- Try not to take over baby care in front of the parents.
  - This can make them feel badly about their ability to cope, and it may cause them to become angry or push you away.
  - Instead, if they are frustrated and asking for help, show them how to hold the baby or burp the baby once and then hand the baby back for them to do it.
  - Teach and promote their confidence.

- Ask. Ask. Ask.
  - "Can I tell people you are pregnant?" "The gender?" "What time would you like him to be home from the walk?" "What can I do to help right now?" "Can I buy some milk or other groceries for you?"

- Remember: Listen. Listen. Listen.
  - Try not to give advice or your opinion unless asked.
  - If it is not lifesaving, maybe it's best to keep your thoughts, and above all, your "helpful" advice, to yourself.

If you feel you must say something, your relationship with the parents will probably determine how they will react, and you need to balance the importance of what you will say and what might happen.

Parent First

Remember, you are still the parent. As such, you are expected to be more patient and wiser. You certainly have more life experience, but you don't know everything. I believe that it is up to you (not your child) to try to lead the way in effective communication and improve it for the sake of your new grandfamily.

If you have done something that has offended and you realize it, then apologize as soon as you can and try to move forward. You don't necessarily have to explain in detail or be defensive. "Sorry" is a word that seems to be slipping from our vocabulary. Apologizing can help mend a hurt and avoid alienation. Take a cooling off time if you need it. Staying open and not getting defensive promotes a good relationship.

> **A young mother told me,** "Mothers today feel bombarded with advice and experts and opinions and choices. It's overwhelming. What we need most is your unconditional love and support."

Even well-meaning comments can feel like criticism to the vulnerable, tired new parent. Dr. Sears' book advises parents who feel criticized to limit exposure and spend time with similar-minded people. This means that you might not get to be with them or the baby, as you would like. It is not worth risking being cut out of your grandfamily's life for even a short time for the sake of being right and failing to acknowledge when you are not.

Dr. Sears also tells parents that they can better cope with criticism from grandparents by being confident and replying, "It's working for us." If you hear that comment from the new parents, you might need to look at their book. It advises new parents that those of us who didn't practice attachment parenting might be threatened by this style of parenting and wish we had followed our instincts. They do tell parents to respect us (and to ask for respect), to try to understand our feelings, and to tell us that they turned out well.

The book also suggests that parents avoid talking about what they call the "big three": discipline, breastfeeding, and bedsharing. These are also the things that grandmothers told me had changed, and even worried them the most, and the things that new parents said was the cause of conflict between them and their parents.

HOW TO HELP

There are things that you can do that many new mothers told me they greatly appreciated from grandparents.

Babysitting

I loved babysitting as a teenager, and I couldn't wait to babysit my grandson. You may or may not look forward to babysitting. The amount of time you spend babysitting can vary from providing actual childcare as some of my friends have done to casual relief when the parents want to go out. As you can expect, there are mutual benefits to babysitting.

For you, you get the little one all to yourself. I

> One grandma, whose daughter is a self-employed professional and returned to work shortly after her baby was born, told me: *"I was happy to provide childcare for Sam, not only to help offset babysitting costs, but also to have more time with him and to avoid having him cared for by a stranger at such a young age. But when my daughter was pregnant again, and assumed that I would babysit two young children, I had to say 'No.'"*
>
> She knew that she needed to avoid burning out. The family got a nanny, Grandma agreed to cover occasional nights out or for emergencies, and it worked out well for everyone.

find I am more relaxed caring for my grandson when we are by ourselves. We have lots of fun, and although I try my hardest to follow their routines, there are bound to be some things that we do a little differently. The best part is you get to be involved in their day-to-day lives.

For the parents, the benefits are numerous: someone whom they know and trust to put their child's needs and safety foremost cares for their child. Once when I was babysitting, my husband brought over dinner for our grandson and us. It was wonderful. I felt like a teenager having my boyfriend over (something I never did at the time).

Whether or not you are working outside the home, your time is important. There may be times when you can manage last-minute requests to watch your grandbaby, and changing lunch with your sister to another day isn't a hardship, but canceling a medical appointment you waited two months for might not be feasible.

Having grandparents babysit is an obvious cost savings. Daily rates vary greatly. My daughter was quite surprised to find out that the hourly rate for teenage babysitters in our area is up to $20 per hour. In addition to the cost of going to a concert or a movie, paying for babysitting can make many new parents think twice about going out on a much needed date night.

Babysitting isn't as carefree as you might think, and just because you are free doesn't mean it is any less serious a commitment:

- Be reliable.

  — If your child asks you to babysit at a certain time, be there as promised. If you are not, it makes it easy for them to feel they have to call someone else next time to care for your grandchild.

  > *Establish your personal boundaries.*

- Check your calendar first and decide if it works for you.

  — Can you really be available at a moment's notice or every Saturday night?

- Safety is paramount.

  — The parents have likely made the latest safety improvements needed in their home as the baby grows, and your house probably hasn't been childproofed for years, or not ever if you have moved.

Their House or Yours

There are pros and cons to caring for your grandchild in your house or at their house. At their house, there is everything baby needs and is familiar to her. However, I must admit that I get bored if my grandson is sleeping, and I feel a little trapped if I have things to do at home.

In my house, I have different toys, some belonging to my children. We listen to music and dance around. I got CDs of the albums that I sang and danced around to with my own children. I ordered new copies of books I read to them. The words and tunes are all familiar and that adds to my comfort and fun. My grandson has liked each one and seems to love me singing along to "Baby Beluga" as much as my children did.

A bonus of babysitting at your house is that you can attend to things while the baby is napping, playing quietly, or "helping" prepare dinner. You can put your laundry in (let your grandchild press the button or put the dryer balls in) or wait for a repairperson! One friend who often cares for her young granddaughters at her house has a crib and a play yard (See–Play Yard) for naptime. They are used to this and readily go in their respective "beds" when Grandma puts them in them.

> **We didn't prepare for our grandson to sleep at our house.**
>
> *When he was very small, I could snuggle with him in the rocking chair or put him in a laundry basket, but he would have to go home for his real nap.*

A friend wanted me to buy a crib to share with her and use when our grandchildren would visit, but we have a small house, so I didn't want to do this. When my grandson was eighteen months old and his parents were busy building their new home, I borrowed the crib from her in the hopes of him having a nap. Because his bedroom at home is quite dark, I put blackouts on my windows. I took him for a walk and, when he was asleep, I gently brought him in the house only to have him wake immediately. I tried cradling him in the rocking chair, but that didn't work; neither did lying in my bed with him. He was quite interested in all this activity, but didn't nap. My daughter took him home and, naturally, he fell asleep in the car and didn't have a good nap afterwards. We have tried a few times since to have him nap in the crib, following all his usual routines at home, but it just hasn't worked.

I strongly suggest that if you plan to babysit in your home, get some equipment, and have the baby sleep at your house on occasion before she might need to.

- Start early so the baby is used to sleeping there.
  - Suggest that the baby have naps at your house when the parents are there to get her used to sleeping there; it will make it much easier when they leave and you put her down.

- Buy or borrow a crib, but make sure it meets safety regulations.
  - Or get a play yard that can be packed away when you don't need it.

- Have a special blanket at your house similar to one the baby likes at her own house, and request that your grandchild come with her favorite sleeping items—blankie, books, and bears.

- Follow routines as best as possible.

Nannies and Childminders

More and more families are getting nannies. The cost of full time child-care and the efforts associated with getting children to daycare early in the morning and picking them up at suppertime add to family stress. The families that I know who have nannies find them to be a godsend. Many keep them even if the mother is on maternity leave with a new baby, to maintain the routine and activities for the other children. Some do housework and meals, but not all. You aren't the boss of the nanny or babysitter or daycare, so you should refer any concerns, unless immediate and life-threatening, to the parents.

Holiday Sitting

Many grandmas I know are invited to fill-in when nanny has holidays or the daycare is unavailable. More desirable might be to take a vacation together; you can share childcare with the parents, relax as a family, and enjoy a holiday. We often see multi-generational families on vacation together.

WHEN A SIBLING COMES ALONG

The public health nurse walked into the house; ignored me and my brand-new daughter, said hello to my two-year-old son, and played with him on the floor. I was put out—didn't she care about the new baby she was here to see? She played with my son for a while and told me to get the baby ready to be weighed without looking up. When my son was content, she asked him to show her "his" baby sister and then checked my daughter. Smart lady!

Toddler Regression

Reverting to more infantile behaviors, such as thumb-sucking or soiling after being toilet trained, can happen whenever there is stress or change, but is most common when a new sibling joins the family of the two-year-old.

> Expect Toddler Regression: It can be hard when everyone is so excited about a new baby. She has been the center of everyone's attention for a few years, and now the parents are busy attending to the baby's needs and her nose can be out of joint!

How you can help

Pay attention to the older siblings first and make them feel like they are still important, especially while the parents care for the new baby. Alternatively, you can change the baby while the parents read or put the older child to bed as they had done in the past. Ignore negative outbursts as best possible, distracting to activities that are more positive works well.

> Be aware that toddlers can easily hurt a new sibling (even if unintentional).
>
> Do not ever leave a toddler alone with a new baby.

When the older child is napping or being cared for by the parents, you can have your turn with the baby. It might be a good time for you to take the older child to a new activity such as swimming class or music group to give the parents' time to rest and bond with the new baby.

Many grandmothers confirmed my belief that having a second baby close to the first is more than twice the work at the beginning for everyone (including grandma), no sooner is one child changed than the other one needs to be. Leaving the house for a walk can take an hour of preparation! Parents (and grandmothers who help) can be exhausted in the first while after a new baby joins the family.

VISITING

One morning I emailed my daughter to say that I would be dropping some things off that she had asked me to get for her. I hadn't wanted to phone in case I woke the baby. She had not received the e-mail I had sent, so she didn't expect me. I rang the doorbell. Both she and

> Do not drop in unannounced!

the baby were in their pajamas when she answered the door, looking like they had just woken up. I felt badly when I realized that she thought I had just dropped in on her.

> When you visit, you don't want to wake the baby announcing yourself.
>
> Gently knock and go in if you have a key. Remember to lock it behind you (in and out) if there are toddlers in the house.

If they know you are coming, it may not be necessary to call, but don't assume that you are always welcome to pop over. just quietly knock. Think how you would have felt with anyone just dropping by unannounced in those first few weeks!

If you are newly retired and suddenly have a lot of time on your hands, do not assume that it can or should all be filled by your grand-family. While it may be excellent for you to help, you need to have a full, healthy life of your own, independent of your grown children and their lives.

IN-LAWS

There is a litany of jokes about the "mother-in-law" or MiL, as we are called now. Movies like *Monster-in-Law* or *Meet the Parents* make good humor out of the in-law relationship, but not all is quite so funny in real life.

As with your daughter, you have a lifetime history of communication and resolving problems with your son. You do not share this history with your daughter-in-law, and your offers of advice and assistance may be received quite differently than from your own child. With this comes the increased potential for hurt feelings and rejection.

Now might be a good time to reflect on your previous interactions and your overall relationship since they became a couple.

> One new mother said, "My MiL wanted to do everything like she was the mom. The worst for me was when Aiden cried and obviously needed me; I would have to ask her to give him to me. It made things awkward and uncomfortable. I ended up asking my husband to intervene so that I wasn't so stressed about it. I felt she thought I should let others soothe him, but there are times only mommy will do, and we knew those times, but she didn't."

- Do you feel as though you are walking on eggshells to avoid offending her or just cannot talk to her openly?

- If there was a wedding, were there areas of conflict in the planning about the wedding?

- Do you sometimes feel unhappy or left out of their lives?

- Do you wish he had married someone else?

If you answered yes, then you might want to tread very carefully before assuming what will unfold as you start to grandmother.

One woman was shocked when her adult son appeared to listen exclusively to his soon-to-be wife about their wedding. She felt cut out of decisions about the ceremony, and her suggestions about the reception were ignored. She was hurt and offended when subsequent life choices were made without her input. She frequently exclaimed, "But I didn't raise him that way!" However, she *did* raise him—that way. She raised a son who watched his father be eternally loving and loyal to his mother, and he observed his mother's negative relationship with her own mother-in-law. Prior to his wife, the major decisions in his life were made by another strong woman—her.

Was it any surprise that her son would marry a woman similar to her in so many ways? I think not. When she heard about the pregnancy, she was worried about how much she would be able to participate in her grandchild's life. Rightfully so.

I have seen plenty of women and their partners cringe when an overbearing mother/mother-in-law comes to visit her new grandchild for the first time in the hospital. Some of these new parents, who were perhaps nervous and proud a few minutes before, just sit in the bed or chair looking desolate as she takes over, holding the baby while visitors look on—she who considers herself an expert about all things baby because she birthed thirty years ago.

> One mother describes her MiL, *"She tries too hard and tries to plan too much, and I wish she would relax and enjoy rather than pushing her own agenda and ideas."*

Then she will lecture and criticize what they have just been taught by us "experts" in the medical field. Their confusion and disappointment are clear.

Some women told me they felt worthless when they heard that their mother or mother-in-law had spoken to their husband about things they thought she was doing wrong with caring for baby, either in front of her or behind her back. Sad indeed.

However, miracles do happen. One new grandmother of a beautiful little boy was surprised at the turn of the tide that happened in her relationship with her DiL (daughter-in-law—we can do it, too!). DiL had gone out with her son for many years in a long-distance relationship. They married once she returned to town, and she got pregnant not long after. The baby is six months old now, and things have changed.

The mother-in-law said, "I just never had much to talk to her about until the baby was born. It was always uncomfortable with long periods of silence. Now we have this same focus for our attention and love—the baby. She (DiL) is very determined in how she cares for the baby, but they love him so much and are doing a great job. I worried about the lack of a soother when the baby was so obviously teething. They gave him a very expensive rubber giraffe to chew on when he was fussy. I wanted him to have a proper teething ring, but I zipped my mouth shut. I looked up this rubber giraffe online, only to discover it is the number one teething toy. I was reassured that they are doing all the right things for him. They really are wonderful parents."

Her face lit up when she told this story. She is obviously so proud of her son and his wife and was thrilled with her unexpected new positive relationship with her daughter-in-law. She was wise to avoid commenting on things they were doing that were so different

> More than one grandmother told me that the baby had improved the relationship with her daughter-in-law or her step-daughter.

from how she had raised her own babies without knowing why. She is an active part of their lives. She visits and gets to care for her grandson as often as she likes.

This can reassure you that even if your relationship with your DiL isn't the strongest right now, it can grow as you both love and care for your grandbaby.

Your Son or Son-in-Law

The role of fathers as parents has changed immensely since we were born, and more so since, we had our children. In most birthing centers today, fathers can (and are expected to) stay with the mother throughout the whole process. Many units offer sleeping cots or mats for the husband or even queen-sized beds for the couple. It is wonderful to see how many fathers embrace the chance to care for their partner and new baby.

You may be pleasantly surprised at your son or son-in-law's knowledge and skills as a new parent. The first week or so, most employers give fathers-to-be time off to attend the birth, and some take time off as either paid or unpaid paternity leave. This means that they can continue to bond as a new family or allow the mother to continue with school or work

My daughter had an emergency C-section and needed help. In those first few weeks while she recovered from the surgery and focused on breastfeeding and pumping, my son-in-law and I were like zombies taking shifts helping with "finger feeding" him expressed breast milk, diaper changes, and maintaining the house. While I could see that he was tired, I never heard him complain. When I questioned him about helping with night feeds and diapers, he smiled and replied, "[She] is with him all day when I am at work. I want to be with him as much as I can, too."

New dads need to be aware of their own limitations; working all day and then caring for their new family when they get home can be exhausting. Recent research has shown that sleep-deprived new fathers are more likely to get in car accidents and have mishaps at work.

The Other Grandparents

There is usually at least one other grandparent in your expanding grandfamily. It can be either a bonding opportunity or a situation in which the differences between the two families become very evident. Worse yet,

> You may want to try to involve the other grandparents in family activities, but if your child does not want them there, you won't be able to.

46

competition for the affection of the child or splitting affection between children can arise. It can be even more complex when there has been divorce, remarriage, and problem relationships that have not healed.

The in-laws may or may not already have other grandchildren. If they are already grandparents, this might give them the edge in terms of baby care and equipment, but they will also be new players in this new grandfamily, and their parenting practices are likely to be unfamiliar.

There can be conflicts in values and experiences with baby care, especially with infant feeding and discipline. If you breastfed your children until they were eighteen months old, you are most likely comfortable with the latest breastfeeding guidelines (two years), but this may seem very odd to the other grandmother(s) if they only nursed for few weeks or bottle-fed their babies. What if the other grandparents smoke (as my parents did)? What if they are never available to help (as with my in-laws) (as some of you may not be able to)?

You can help your grandchildren by doing the following:

- Refrain from saying negative things or prying the child about her relationship with other grandparents.

- Appreciate that children and grandchildren thrive with love and that you aren't the only grandparent able to provide it.

- Include the other grandparents in family activities.

- Try to put aside your differences—the children and grandchildren are more important than issues between the two of you.

Step-Grandmother

Divorce, death, and remarriage all make for complex family situations, with some children having many people who fit into the grandparent category. From what I have seen, most young children adapt very well to these different people in their lives, as long as the children feel that the person cares about them. It seems to be more difficult for the adults, who can hold grudges against ex-spouses or new ones.

> One stepmother with no biological grandchildren suggests,
>
> *"Even if you are not a primary grandmother, try to remain supportive and available."*

Children can have multiple grandparents either directly or indirectly related to them. The upside is that many children these days are blessed with multiple sets and combinations of grandparents. If the children are part of your child's life, it follows that they are now part of yours.

One woman's son recently married a woman with two young sons. Because she knew these boys would be part of her grandfamily, she made a point to send and make them special gifts at the holidays and just out of the blue to let them know that she and "Grandpa" are thinking of them. This wise, engaged, grandma advises other step-grandmothers to do the following:

- Make the children feel special and part of your family; let them see you trying.
  - Treat them the same way you treat any other grandchildren you have.
  - Go out of your way to include the step-grandchild in family events.
  - Buy or make special gifts and foods they like.

As with other relationships, this can depend a lot on previous encounters. If the step-grandmother doesn't have a close relationship with the parent, it may or may not be an opportunity to become closer. Realize that if the new mother has a mother she is close to or if there are a grandmother and a step-grandmother on the father's side, your involvement might not be as great as you might hope, but there are many years for a relationship to form and other grandchildren will likely come along soon enough.

FINANCIAL SUPPORT

Gift cards to maternity or baby shops might be well received.

Offer to go shopping with her and you can get ideas for what they need and would appreciate.

In 2004, the estimated cost to raise a child varied, from $160,000 in Canada to more than $250,000 in the United States, including college tuition.

Finances are one area with which you may be in a position

to help your child and grandfamily. Your own finances are more than likely to be more secure now than when your children were little, and this may give you an opportunity to make a significant difference in the future of your grandchild without appearing that you are meddling in your children's parenting.

Educational plans

I contributed to an education plan for both of my children. When it matured, the amount that was advised by the plan was woefully inadequate to buy the textbooks. Ask your child first; but, as a grandparent, if you have the means, you will likely be able to contribute to an education savings plan for your grandchildren. There are a variety of different education plans in the United States and Canada. You need to check with your banker or financial planner to determine the best option for both you and your grandfamily. These are the major plans.

In the United States:

- A 529 plan is a government, tax-advantaged plan that encourages saving to meet the higher-education expenses of a designated beneficiary: http://www.savingforcollege.com/intro_to_529s/name-the-top-7-benefits-of-529-plans.php.

- Depending on the state, there can be matching scholarship and grant opportunities.

- There are prepaid tuition credit plans or savings plans that grow with the market.

In Canada:

- You can contribute each year to a Registered Education Savings Plan (RESP).

- The baby will need a Social Insurance Number (parents apply for this) to apply.

- The plan can be registered through the parents' banking institution or one of a few private companies offering the plans.

— This way, the parents can manage it, apply for government matching grants, and access the money when the child is ready to use it.

• The maximum you can deposit is $5,000 each year, but with a deposit of $2,500, the government will also contribute an additional 20 percent (maximum $500) in the form of a Canada Education Savings Grant and some provinces an additional 10 percent.

• At this time, the maximum amount that can be deposited tax-free is $36,000: http://www.cra-arc.gc.ca/tx/ndvdls/tpcs/resp-reee/menu-eng.html?=slnk http://www.hrsdc.gc.ca/eng/learning/education_savings/public/resp.shtml http://www.publications.gov.sk.ca/details.cfm?p=66324.

Insurance

Some companies advertise to try to get parents and grandparents to buy life insurance for young children. Insurance is intended to replace income and security; babies do not usually provide an income, so for most families, there is nothing to replace or insure should the child die. The cost can be low for the policy. There is a benefit to being able to transfer to a larger policy when the child grows, but there may be costs associated with doing so. The company that I see advertising most on television states on its website that it will be using/sharing your information with other companies, so be careful with such plans.

> *There are many ways you can support your child and grandchildren. Find a way that works for all of you.*

4. Pregnancy Today

A pregnant woman in the family is marvelous, but as I recently told a new grandmother-to-be, for you this is lesson number one: As excited as you may be, it is not your news to share. Ask your child if you can tell people, and be true to what they say they want you to do.

Some parents want to tell everyone about the pregnancy right away; others do not tell before the end of the first trimester, especially if there is concern about loss of the baby or previous pregnancy disappointments. If the woman is feeling very nauseated or is suddenly not drinking alcohol, those around her will likely notice and question if she is pregnant, and it's up to her how to answer, but sometimes your expression will give you away!

> Pregnancy is now a couples' event. You are likely to hear your daughter or daughter-in-law and partner say, "We're pregnant."

It is unfortunate when a woman feels she has to keep her pregnancy quiet and then if she is having a challenging pregnancy or if she does lose the baby, she may not get the support she will need. Also, you are more likely to be sympathetic with emotional turmoil or canceled visits if you know she is pregnant.

I know some people are superstitious about having the shower or giving gifts before the baby is born, but this isn't how things are done anymore. Baby showers are often co-ed now; with partners there, with potluck, although the silly games seem to have endured!

> If someone asks if your child or child's partner is pregnant, and you are silent, it will be obvious. *Instead, you might say, "That would be lovely wouldn't it?"*

Parents need items before the baby is born, and we now see showers being held anytime. Some women register their baby at various department stores and toy stores, so you might have to ask for a list of all the places and share that information with others.

CONCEPTION

How they conceive or become pregnant may well be new to you if it includes assisted reproductive technology (ART). You may never know the details of how the event happened. Some women spend years building their careers. As they age, they ovulate less regularly and may need help to conceive. Women with medical disorders such as polycystic ovary disease also can have a hard time getting pregnant.

International and older-child adoptions are increasingly popular, but are not the answer for everyone. Children today can be conceived in different ways:

Assisted Reproductive Technology (ART)

ART involves any fertility techniques than involve the egg and/or sperm.

- Women may have their ovaries stimulated by injected medications to produce eggs, and a number of them may be "harvested" (removal of eggs from the woman's ovary, usually via an opening made in the vagina).

- The eggs are combined with sperm in various methods and put back into her or into another woman (a surrogate).

Surrogacy: Surrogates are women who become pregnant and give birth to a baby for another person.

- Surrogates can become pregnant with a harvested egg, but some donate their own eggs, which may have been fertilized by the father's sperm or donor sperm.

- Some couples will go to another country to have a woman there carry their baby for them.

- In many countries, there are strict laws around "hiring" or paying surrogates.

> If they do tell you what is happening, find out what you can about whatever method they have chosen.
>
> *Go online to a reputable site (See–Resources) or ask your gynecologist.*

Artificial Insemination: Sperm from either the partner or a donor are inserted into the vagina or directly into the uterus. The woman's cycle may need to be regulated or stimulated with medication.

In Vitro Fertilization (IVF): In vitro means "outside the body." The egg and sperm are brought together outside the woman's body for fertilization. The zygote or embryo is then inserted inside the mother's or surrogate's fallopian tube, uterus, or vagina.

Egg Donation: If the woman is older or has other genetic concerns, she may have an egg donated and fertilized with her partner's or a donor's sperm and she may carry the baby herself.

All of these procedures can be exhausting, expensive, and stressful, usually after many years of trying to conceive. Many are not successful the first time or even the first few times. For instance, IVF has a 12 to 25 percent success rate—lower with the advancing age of the mother. If you know that your child and partner are going through any of these artificial reproductive methods, they will need your support.

Gestation

Pregnancy, or gestation, is the carrying of a fetus until its birth. Usual human gestation is forty weeks long (not nine months), and women these days are much more likely to tell you how many weeks pregnant they are instead of months.

> *Any time a baby is born before or after term, there is a potential for health problems.*

Pregnancy is divided into trimesters: the first trimester is up to thirteen weeks' gestation, the second is up to twenty-six weeks, and the third trimester continues until the fetus is born. Ideally, babies are born at "term," between thirty-seven and forty-two weeks' gestation.

- Babies born before thirty-seven weeks are called "preterm"; rarely do you hear the word "premature" anymore.
  - The age of the baby and the baby's overall wellbeing, determine her chances of surviving and her long-term health.
  - We have all seen pictures of very tiny babies in incubators. They are vulnerable to breathing, blood circulation, infection, heart function, and digestion problems in the early period and challenges to their wellbeing over time.
- Babies born at thirty-four to thirty-seven weeks are called "late preterm babies."
  - Some late preterm babies may weigh five pounds or more, but they are still at risk for breathing, temperature regulation, infection, and eating problems despite their size and appearance.
- Babies born after forty-two weeks are "postdates" or "postmature."
  - The longer a baby remains in the womb after forty-two weeks, the higher the chances of stillbirth and of the woman being induced for labor.

Multiples

Mothers are waiting longer to have their children, with this comes a greater chance of having multiples, i.e., twins or more! A lifelong friend sent me a Christmas card, pleased she was becoming a grandmother. Shortly afterwards I got a birthday card, saying there were triplets! She knew that this meant her daughter and husband would need help, but she recognized her limitations with her own health challenges and felt badly that she couldn't give the physical help and support she knew was going to be needed.

Parents of multiples may face greater financial strain; the mother may have had to finish work sooner than expected or may be hospitalized during the pregnancy; it can be especially burdensome if there are other children. Buying furnishings, equipment, and ongoing supplies can feel overwhelming for them. Additionally, the babies are more likely to be born early or have health problems, so your extra arms (and your husband's) are likely to be needed more than the parents anticipate.

TESTS

Women have many blood tests during pregnancy, including for anomalies (such as defects that involve the spine). High levels of certain proteins and hormones might indicate an anomaly. If there is an indication of some problem, further testing by an amniocentesis (needle inserted into womb and fluid removed) may be needed to evaluate the baby's cells for genetic and other problems. This is especially important in women over thirty-five years, who are at higher risk for Down's and other syndromes.

Ultrasound

You may have had an ultrasound (U/S) in your pregnancies. U/S is a test that is often, but not always, done during pregnancy. It uses high-frequency sound waves we cannot hear. These waves are transmitted through the abdomen via a "transducer," and the echoes are recorded and transformed into either a video or a photographic image of the baby or her heart rate.

First-Trimester Ultrasounds: Done at around six weeks, to confirm the pregnancy, check the number of fetuses, and get an early estimation of the due date.

- They may be done through the abdomen or with a vaginal probe.

Second-Trimester Ultrasounds: Done at around eighteen weeks primarily to assess growth, development, and the position of placenta and baby.

- They can detect signs of anomalies such as Down syndrome or heart defects.

- May be possible to determine the gender. Not all parents want to know and may not tell you if they do find out.

Like many couples, my daughter and her husband did find out the gender of their first baby at ultrasound. We met for lunch, and they proudly announced it was a boy! I must admit, this made shopping and gift making much more fun, especially because even the neutral clothes (white, yellow, and green) often have a bit of gender-specific design on them.

As nice as it is to know the gender, before you help paint the nursery or buy pink sleepers, you need to know that errors can occur with ultrasound. Even with amniocentesis, findings are written down or reported in error, to the surprise, and sometimes disappointment, of everyone.

> My second grandbaby had its legs crossed, so gender couldn't be determined as early, but we were reassured of its health. The later ultrasound was done on my birthday and his parents gave me blue hydrangeas to indicate I had another grandson.

Third-Trimester Ultrasounds: Done to assess ongoing growth and position of placenta and baby.

- These are important especially if there are concerns about the pregnancy (e.g., preterm labor, postdates, diabetes in the mother).

- They also may also have a special test to assess the baby's wellbeing as the pregnancy progresses, especially if the baby isn't growing. It is called a biophysical profile (BPP).

- If there are concerns about the baby's health or development, a "detailed" or "advanced scan" will be done of her internal organs (e.g., lungs, heart, and kidneys) or the skeleton, especially the spine.
  - This can be very stressful for the parents (and grandparents).

- Parents may also pay for a detailed 3D or 4D ultrasound offered by private companies.
  - They will likely provide pictures and a DVD of the baby and report the baby's gender.

— Sadly, there are reports of parents using this method to select the gender of the baby and terminate the pregnancy if the baby is not the desired gender. Some places are looking at monitoring their use. The cost is usually a hundred dollars or more.

PREGNANCY HEALTH

Pregnancy is a wonderful experience for most women, but there can be health challenges that are good to know about.

Nausea and Vomiting

Most women experience some nausea and vomiting in pregnancy (NVP) or morning sickness in the first trimester. NVP is often the sign of a healthy pregnancy, caused by increasing and new hormones being produced in her body, but it can also be horrible for the woman experiencing it. In severe situations, I have seen women vomit bile and be admitted to the hospital for rehydration and electrolytes. For some women NVP can last until the baby is born. People worry about the effects of NVP on the baby, but babies seem to fare well, and there is research showing that children of mothers with NVP have high intelligence!

Vitamins, especially those that contain iron, can increase NVP and can cause other stomach and bowel problems. But, there are things that can help:

• If the woman is made sick by taking vitamins, she can stop taking them and try again later in the pregnancy when the nausea and vomiting have subsided, or she can try taking one with reduced or no iron.

• Encourage her to try to take the folic acid.

• There are many suggested remedies, including dry crackers, ginger, and special pressure point bracelets.

• Take her to a clinic or emergency for hydration, if NVP is severe.

• Be sensitive to how perfumes and other odours can cause nausea.

- One medication, Diclectin, is approved for NVP.

  — A woman who had NVP in one pregnancy is likely to have it again, and she is advised to take the medication early in the pregnancy for the best effect.

- Motherisk in Toronto, Canada offers a NVP help phone line (1-800-436-8477: http://www.motherisk.org/women/morningSickness.jsp).

> "Women are encouraged to take prenatal vitamins three months before they become pregnant. To take them while pregnant, and continue until the bottle is empty after the baby is born"

Vitamins

As you probably did, most pregnant women take a special prenatal vitamin. Prenatal vitamins usually contain more calcium, iron, and folic acid and less Vitamin A than regular adult vitamins.

Many of us are low in Vitamin D. Everyone needs Vitamin D for bone growth, but it is also associated with increased immunity and overall wellbeing.

- Pregnant women are advised to take 600 IU (international units) of Vitamin D a day; most prenatal vitamins provide this amount.

Folic Acid (Folate)

Vitamin B9 [folic acid (a supplement) or folate (naturally occurring in food)] is essential to prevent brain, skull, and spinal problems such as spina bifida (a condition in which the spine and spinal column do not fuse as usually occurs in the first month of uterine life). Therefore, pregnant women are advised to:

> Seeing a bottle of folic acid or prenatal vitamins can be an indication that a couple is trying to conceive or pregnant.

- Take prenatal vitamins containing folic acid, or take folic acid separately if she cannot tolerate the entire vitamin.

- Take up to 0.4 mg [400 micrograms (mcg)] of folic acid daily for the three months before becoming pregnant and for at least the first three months of the pregnancy. If possible, it is best for her to take it consistently throughout pregnancy.

- Not take more than 1.0 mg of folic acid each day.

Women who have a postpartum hemorrhage are often told to continue to take 0.4 mg of folic acid along with an iron supplement or to take their prenatal vitamins for the first six months postpartum to promote the development of new red blood cells.

Folate/folic acid is also found in various foods, but women continue to take a supplement to ensure that they get an adequate amount.

- Dark green vegetables (such as broccoli, brussel sprouts, peas, and spinach), corn, dried peas, beans, lentils, oranges, and orange juice all provide a good source of folate.

- Enrichment of bread products with folic acid has been mandatory in the United States and Canada since the 1990s.

Weight

Weight is a very sensitive topic, and pregnancy doesn't change that. I gained a lot of weight with my first pregnancy. I have blocked out the exact amount, but what I do remember is that my ex-father-in-law (who often made snide weight-related comments) made a nasty remark about me weighing as much as he did. I have looked at pictures of myself around that time of my pregnancy, and I see a healthy pregnant young woman, nothing remotely close to his 250 pounds. I have no idea why he said what he did, but it was very hurtful and made me feel self-conscious.

My mother told me that they wore girdles until they couldn't do so anymore, to try to keep from appearing pregnant. Some women use smoking to minimize weight gain and to stifle the baby's size, hoping for easier deliveries!

Normal Weight Gain

Normal weight gain in pregnancy is twenty-five to thirty-five pounds. Women are not literally "eating for two", as you and she might have been told by some well-meaning, but uninformed people. Rather, pregnant women need to eat an additional 350 to 500 calories or an extra snack or two a day after the first trimester.

> **Expected weight gain includes the following:**
>
> • *Baby: ~7.5 lbs.*
> • *Extra blood, fluids, protein: ~7.5 lbs.*
> • *Breasts and energy stores: ~6.5 lbs.*
> • *Uterus: ~2 lbs.*
> • *Placenta: ~2 lbs.*
> • *Amniotic fluid: ~2 lbs.*

Proper pregnancy weight gain differs with her pre-pregnant body mass index (BMI). BMI is a measure of body fat based on a person's height and weight. It can be calculated online at sites like http://www.nhlbi.nih.gov/guidelines/obesity/BMI/bmicalc.htm. For a woman pregnant with one baby, the following weight gain is suggested:

> **The news is full of celebrities losing their "baby weight" soon after delivering. This can put pressure on women not to gain adequate weight so that they, too, can look like they have not been pregnant.**
>
> *I do not know how they lose their weight or have flat tummies so quickly. Perhaps with personal trainers, chefs, and surgical interventions that average women cannot afford.*

• Underweight women (BMI less than 18.5) can gain up to 40 lbs.

• Overweight women (BMI of 25 to 29.9) are advised to gain 15–25 lbs.

• Obese women (BMI greater than 30) need to try to keep their weight gain to no more than 20 lbs.

My first pregnancy was an opportunity to enjoy my favorite foods like ice cream and chocolate pudding—without reserve. I did lose the extra weight, but it was work. With my next pregnancy, between running around after a toddler and the hard work of losing the weight before, I gained much less and found it was much easier to lose postpartum.

Weight issues

Your daughter or daughter-in-law may already have struggles with her weight or have body-image problems before pregnancy. This can be a worrisome time for women with eating disorders or eating problems (such as anorexia or bulimia/vomiting). Recognize that your role is to support her health and that of the baby, while maintaining the relationship. Try not to be or appear critical.

- Perhaps say nothing at all, especially if she has weight issues (too much or too little). If she asks, reassure her.

> Do not brag about coming home from the hospital after your third child wearing your pre-pregnancy jeans!
>
> *It will not help the new mother or your relationship with her.*

- Keep healthful foods around your house; find out what she likes and take the couple healthy meals to eat.

- Ask her what she would like to eat when you are preparing meals.

- Do not ridicule her food cravings and aversions.

- Do not try to force her to eat when she says she is not hungry or try to make her eat high-calorie foods, worse yet, "eat for two."

- Respect her food habits.

  - If she was an octo-lacto-vegetarian before she became pregnant, she is likely to try to manage the same diet during pregnancy and breastfeeding.

  - It can be a challenge for her to get all of the nutrients she needs, but she is likely very familiar with her dietary needs and will look at the changes she needs to make with her food choices and may need to supplement her diet.

- Don't cook foods that are very smelly or greasy.

- Fish is an excellent source of protein, vitamins, and omega fatty acids, all essential for the developing fetus. However, due to high levels of methylmercury, women are advised not to have more than 12 ounces of canned tuna, salmon, shrimp, pollock, or catfish per week. There are fish that pregnant women need to avoid altogether, such as shark and grouper.

— A detailed article about the fish and shellfish and childbearing women is available at http://www.fda.gov/food/foodsafety/product-specificinformation/seafood/foodborne pathogenscontaminants/methylmercury/ucm115662.htm.

Obesity

Being overweight or obese can lead to fertility problems for the couple and ongoing problems for the woman and her baby.

- Babies of obese mothers can be born larger than average, leading to more use of forceps, the possibility of the baby's shoulders getting stuck during delivery (shoulder dystocia), and a higher chance of a Cesarean (C-section) (note, many C-sections have nothing to do with mother's weight gain).

  — The obese mother is more likely to have an infection, especially if she has a C-section.

- Obesity puts the woman at increased risk for gestational diabetes (diabetes that starts in pregnancy).

> **Be considerate.**
>
> *Make healthy meals you know she will enjoy and the whole family will eat.*

  — Her babies are at increased risk for being large for their age, have respiratory problems, jaundice, and their own blood sugar problems.

  — She is more likely to develop diabetes later in life (when she becomes a grandmother!)

- Obese women are also more likely to have gestational (during pregnancy) hypertension and pre-eclampsia, which can lead to preterm delivery and ongoing health problems for the mother.

Infections

Group B streptococcal septicemia (GBS) is an infection that deserves special mention. Babies can die if infected. The bacteria are found in the vaginas, bowels, or urinary tracts of fifty percent of all women. It is easily spread to the baby during birth.

Pregnant women usually get a vaginal and/or anal swab to screen for GBS at about thirty-five to thirty-seven weeks' gestation. If she is GBS-positive, she will be treated with antibiotics while in labor. If her GBS status isn't known, they will likely treat her. There is no need to treat before labor because GBS can return before the birth.

Babies also can get GBS from other care providers in the first few months because no one knows if they have GBS unless swabbed. Therefore, we all need to wash hands after we use the bathroom and before we handle the baby.

> I had more colds this past winter than I am used to; a friend told me that when her grandchildren were young and started attending activities with other children they all had more colds, too.

Infections and the flu put the pregnant woman and baby at risk. During the SARS (Severe Acute Respiratory Syndrome) and H1N1 (bird) flu outbreaks, pregnant women and newborn babies were most vulnerable to these potentially fatal infections. A breast-fed baby will have increased immunity, but all babies have immature immune systems, and everyone must help protect them.

Flu Shot

All pregnant and postpartum women are encouraged to get the flu shot. However, not all childbearing women do. They worry about getting the flu from the vaccine or worry that the side effects will be harmful to the baby. There is presently no sign of harm to mother or baby from the flu shot.

Getting the flu shot is increasingly important to the health of the mother as the pregnancy progresses. Her immune system can be

> The most important things you can do to help protect your grandfamily from infection are:
>
> 1. Wash your hands often and before handling the baby.
> 2. If you are sick, stay away.
> 3. Encourage the mother to breastfeed.
> 4. Keep your flu shot and other immunizations and vaccinations up-to-date. (especially, whooping cough).

compromised if she gets the flu, and her expanding abdomen can decrease the ability of her lungs to expand. One recent study reported twice the rate of autism in the children of mothers who had the flu, not the flu shot, the flu.

WHEN TO WORRY

There are times when you may be asked about a situation or condition that is new to you, and there are times for everyone to worry about either baby or mother.

The Baby

When I was about eight months pregnant with my first baby, my husband went fishing. I was puttering around the house, which was ten miles out of town and from the hospital. I suddenly realized that I hadn't felt the baby move for a long time. I lay down on my left side to stimulate a kick (lying on the left side, increases blood flow to the baby compared to lying flat). I felt nothing.

Tears streaming down my face, I went out to the car to take myself to the hospital where I worked as an obstetrical nurse. I was sure that my baby was dead. There were no cell phones or radios out on the boat, so I was alone. My 1978 Honda Accord was a very low car and I am very short-waisted. As soon as I got in and crammed myself into the driver's seat, I felt a large kick in the ribs. Relieved, I went back into the house and cried again.

> A friend was not so lucky. Her blood pressure was high. She was advised to be on bedrest at home and to take her blood pressure and monitor the baby's movements.
>
> One day, late in pregnancy, she noticed that the baby wasn't moving. Sadly, by the time she got to the hospital, the baby had no heartbeat.

Movement: Movement is an important indicator of an unborn baby's (fetus) wellbeing.

- A healthy fetus moves often and has short sleep (nap) cycles.

  — The mother usually feels the movement around twenty weeks gestation with the first baby, usually a few weeks earlier if it is not her first baby. The first movement is called "quickening."

- The doctor or midwife will likely tell the woman to count the baby's movements in the morning.

  — Generally, if, after the twenty-sixth week, there have been less than six distinct movements in two hours, the mother needs to go to the nearest hospital.

- If a pregnant woman says that she hasn't felt the baby move for a while, and she hasn't been told what to do, ask her to lie down on her left side (which maximizes blood flow to the baby) and see if that makes a difference.

  — If changing position does not cause the baby to move, then make sure she gets to a hospital for proper medical assessment right away.

  — She can try drinking water, but avoid any food or other liquid in case she needs a C-section.

Heartbeat: Hearing the baby's heartbeat is a wonderful experience for the parents. Babies' hearts are usually formed by six and a half to seven weeks. The heartbeat can be detected by Dopplers or ultrasound, but babies move around a lot, and until the uterus is up out of the pelvic cavity, it can be hard to hear the heartbeat reliably.

- A normal baby's heart beats 110 to 160 beats per minute (bpm). This is much higher than the mother's pulse (60 to 90 bpm). Sometimes these two can be confused, especially if an inexperienced person is trying find it, the woman is obese, the placenta is forward in the uterus, or the baby is in an unusual position.

  — This is important to know because not finding the heartbeat right away can cause a lot of anxiety for the parents. While you will be worried, it is good to show your support. You can be concerned (as you would be), but try not to show your panic.

- The mother may be sent for an ultrasound or may go back to her care provider for another appointment.

The Mother

Most women are healthy in pregnancy; some even "glow," but not all do. The pregnant woman in your life needs to be assessed if she says she:

- Is bleeding.

- Has a sudden gush of fluid vaginally.

- Is seeing spots.

- Has a severe headache.

- Has pain in her upper left abdomen.

- Has gained more than two pounds in a day (may indicate pre-eclampsia or hypertension).

- Has any sign of infection, unusual vaginal discharge (green or foul/fishy smelling). White discharge, leucorrhea, is considered normal.

INFORMATION (OVERLOAD)

Once a woman becomes pregnant, the information and suggestions for her health and that of the baby are never ending. I searched Amazon.com a while ago. There were 145,335 book about "baby", it increased by 30,000 in 10 months; "baby care" increased to 52,770, and "pregnancy" was the focus of 33,794. I am sure there are thousands more already. Talk about overload! This does not even count the advice of well-meaning friends and relatives.

Prenatal Classes

Classes seem to be shorter now and may be held on weekends. Now it's more likely to be a crash course in everything related to the birth, breastfeeding, and the baby.

> One mother told me, *"One thing my mom would say, that I agree with, is that this generation of parents is 'over-educated' about everything. There's so much online, so many theories—it's hard to keep up. This has its pros and cons, and you don't know, at the end of the day, if you're actually learning the best way to be a good parent to your baby."*

Online

Here is one good website that expectant and new parents (and grandparents) might use:

- Baby Center http://www.babycenter.com or http://www.babycenter.ca are online resources that you and your child may find helpful. They offer week-by-week updates and pregnancy calendars with information about fetal development and pregnancy symptoms.

  > Enter details about the baby (due date or birth date) on these sites and you will get emails about what to expect.

  — There are also baby and toddler versions to keep up with information over the years.

- There are many different online sites, some offered by formula and other baby merchandising companies. Many non-government sites appear to have a lot of advertising.

Social Media

It is very likely that your child's friends are also pregnant, thinking of it, or had a baby recently. They are probably sharing what is going on for them.

- Ask your child how their friends are coping and what is happening with them. You might learn about what they plan to do.

Health Care Providers

There is an assortment of care providers and professionals involved in childbearing; unfortunately, they too often offer conflicting advice. The main players include family doctors, obstetricians, midwives, lactation consultants, nurses, and doulas.

Family doctors: Some family doctors will follow the family from pregnancy until after the baby is born and throughout the family's life span. Others only provide pre- and postnatal support, transferring the birth to an obstetrician or another family doctor/midwife for delivery.

Obstetricians: Obstetricians are specialized doctors who are used primarily for medically high-risk pregnancies and usually require a referral from a family doctor or midwife.

Midwives: Midwives are becoming more available, but there may be a waiting list or a cost for private access in some places. It is important that the midwife work within a team so that there is easy access to emergency and specialist care.

Lactation Consultants (LC): LC's are specialists who provide breast-feeding information and support. They work in hospitals or in the community. LC's may or may not be nurses or other health professionals.

- Look for someone who has the IBCLC (International Board Certified Lactation Consultant) qualification.

Nurses: Nurses will likely be there in various roles. While most are well meaning and know a lot about how to help the new family, as with other professionals, not all balance their personal experience with the practice guidelines.

Doulas: The doula may be a new concept to you, but many couples are hiring them to provide emotional and comfort support. The word "doula" comes from the ancient Greek word "servant" or "slave."

- Doulas can be invaluable for families with no experience with babies or when there isn't anyone to support the woman and her partner.

- They may or may not have formal training, and unlike doctors, nurses, and midwives, they do not have a professional association with standards of practice and ethics to oversee their practice.

- Costs vary depending on the services offered. Health insurance plans usually do not cover them.

Although they are not to give clinical advice, I have heard mothers repeat what their doula told them to do, which may not be what their doctor or midwife would advise, such as taking castor oil to induce labor or delaying going to the hospital while in active labor and then delivering unexpectedly at home.

> **Be open to learn.**
>
> *Show your desire to do things the way parents want them done and be the grandmother your family wants and needs.*

5. Labor and Birthing Today

Grandmothers are much more likely to be part of the mother's support group now, that includes in labor, so you need to know more about the process and the care she will likely receive these days.

Process

Every labor is the result of four p's. There isn't much you can do about the first three: the **passage** (her pelvis and other reproductive parts), the **passenger** (the baby—some babies want to come out bum first or with their head in a difficult presentation), and the **powers** (the effectiveness of her contractions). The fourth p is something you might be able to help with—the **psyche**.

While the pain of labor (it's called "labor" because it is hard work) and delivery process are biologically the same as they were when you had your babies, there has been a lot of change in how labor and childbirth are handled.

Hospitals are increasingly likely to have Labor and Birth units (not usually called Delivery units anymore) where the woman is in one room from admission to discharge rather than separate labor, delivery, and postpartum rooms on different floors of the hospital. A nice consequence is that women are rarely moved onto stretchers fully dilated with people yelling at them not to push, then told to roll onto a hard, cold delivery table!

Women are now encouraged to stay at home to labor as long as possible so long as the baby is healthy, the "membranes are not ruptured" (meaning that the amniotic sac/"water" hasn't broken), and there are no other complications (like bleeding or a breech presentation—a bumfirst or feet-first baby). This may be due to hospital bed or staff shortages, but also there is benefit to the woman to staying home. She is more likely to be up walking around and may be better able to manage the discomforts of early labor if she is in her own home.

> Each woman who has given birth has a story to tell. While your daughter or daughter-in-law is in labor is not the time to brag that your baby was born so quickly the doctor barely made it to the birth.
>
> *And it is not helpful to tell the new mother who just needed a C-section or had a bad tear how you had no stitches, unless it is to offer your support for her pain.*

Whatever directions the doctor or midwife gives about going to the hospital, you can know and assure the parents-to-be of the following facts:

- There is no harm in going to the hospital or birthing center for an assessment of the woman and baby.
    - She may feel embarrassed if she goes and finds out that all is well for herself (e.g., normal blood pressure, no bleeding) and the baby (e.g., normal heart rate), her cervix has not dilated, her water hasn't broken, and she ends up being sent home.
    - Assure her that this happens all the time.

- She can try a warm shower
    - If she is in labor, it will feel good and may stimulate contractions; if labor is false, it will likely slow it right down.

- Some hospitals have pre-labor units where she is assessed and then sent home or to somewhere close by.

- Usually a woman must be in active labor before they admit her to the regular birthing unit, but this depends on the facility.

- If she is postdates or there is any indication of problems for the mother or baby, she will be admitted.
  - She may be observed for longer or an induction might be started.

BEING THERE

You may or may not be invited or even permitted to be in the labor or birthing room or even at home if the delivery is there. Maternity wards still have waiting rooms, so you might have to be comfortable with other grandparents there.

- As much as you want to see the baby being born, this is a very intimate time for the couple, and they might not want anyone but the necessary health professionals in the room.

Each institution has its own rules about who and how many can be where and at what time. They may limit the number of people in the room. Some hospitals have rules about the use of cell phones in various spaces, but you ought to be able to stay in good communication even if you aren't in the room.

> One grandmother who had had a rocky relationship with her DiL told me, "*I hoped to be there for the birth. I didn't ask outright; I visited quietly bringing meals and helping with chores in the last week before the baby was born. When things started to happen, my daughter-in-law said, 'Are you coming?' and off we went. It was absolutely transforming.*" They are a closer family now.

- Your relationship with your daughter or daughter-in-law may determine your presence in the labor or birthing room.

- When the mother-to-be is in active labor is not the time to make a fuss about being in the birthing room.

Realize that as a grandmother, you are only one of a potentially large number of people involved, and others may be more essential to the immediate health of the mother and baby than you are.

- If the mother has a partner and a doula, that is already two people. This might be all that is allowed.

> If you are fortunate to be in the room and if there is opportunity, you can quietly reassure her that she is doing a great job, try to understand what is happening around you, or hold her hand.
>
> Try not to be intrusive to the parents or the team.

— You may be able to visit for short periods or fill in during breaks if you stay close by.

• If there are complications, this can increase the number of people who need to be in the room and will likely limit your chances of being present.

- If the mother has a C-section, usually only the father is permitted in the operating room. Sometimes other significant people, like you, can be in a recovery area to see the baby soon after birth, but remember his priority is to be with his partner and newborn.

Home Birth

Your personal values may be challenged by the thought of your grandchild being born at home, but there is a resurgence of this option. It is most important that whoever is attending the birth is qualified (i.e., a certified midwife), has all the necessary equipment and arrangements for possible complications for the mother or baby are made.

The parents and their care providers ultimately determine the type and place of the birth. You can let them know you are available to help wherever the baby is born.

Water Birth

Water births are increasingly popular in home and hospital births alike. Taking warm showers or soaking in a tub can provide pain relief and relaxation, and many think it shortens labor. If a woman is in false labor, it can help ease the contractions.

- There are different kinds of special birthing tubs or pools with or without heaters.

- The birth can happen accidentally in the tub, or it may be planned as a water birth.

- Partners and birth attendants may also get in the pool.

> **From an old obstetrical nurse:**
> *"Mother and baby safety are our goal. As a grandmother, your opinions about their choices, from pain control to method of delivery are best kept to yourself unless asked."*

Induction of Birth

Most babies are born spontaneously, without any medical intervention, but sometimes there is the need to induce labor. At about 41½ weeks' gestation, it is likely that the care provider will plan to "prepare the cervix" and induce labour. Some procedures may be new to you:

Ripening of the Cervix: Although you may have been induced, it is unlikely that you experienced "ripening of the cervix" (to soften and open the cervix).

- A tampon-like product containing prostaglandins or estrogen is inserted into the upper part of the vagina.

- If she lives close, she may go home and wait for labor to start.

- She will be told to monitor the baby's movements and any SoL (Signs of Labor), contractions, bleeding, whether or not the membranes rupture) and call at regular intervals.

Stripping or Sweeping of the Membranes: Some care providers still try to "sweep or strip" the membranes to stimulate labor. A finger is inserted between the membranes (bag of water) and the cervix.

Once the membranes are stripped, the woman needs to:

> *In my experience, this does not hurt any more than a deep pelvic exam.*

- Monitor the baby's movements and regularity of contractions, the presence of blood, and signs that the membranes have ruptured (waters have broken) and to notify her care provider or go to the birth centre when any of these happens.

Rupturing of the Membranes: Once she is in active labor, the membranes either rupture spontaneously—by themselves (SRM) or are ruptured artificially by the doctor or midwife (ARM) using what looks like a long crochet hook.

- There is always a concern that the umbilical cord will fall into the birth canal or will be trapped between the head or shoulder and the pelvis when the membranes rupture.

  — The baby's heart rate needs to be assessed to ensure all is well.

- If the amniotic fluid is green, the woman must seek medical attention immediately because this may indicate that the baby has been stressed and needs to be monitored.

- People are often surprised by the amount of amniotic fluid that is released.

  — "Dry birth" is a myth—in a healthy pregnancy and fetus, amniotic fluid will continue to be produced even after the membranes are ruptured. But due to the increased risk of infection, action will be taken within 24 hours in a term pregnancy.

Oxytocin Induction: What hasn't changed much is an actual induction itself. We still use a synthetic form of oxytocin (also known as Pitocin or Syntocinon). Oxytocin is secreted by the pituitary gland, which then causes uterine contractions. You may have put Pitocin in your mouth beside your cheek.

- Oxytocin is given by an intravenous (IV) pump.

- Women can be induced for a few days in a row depending on her and her baby's health and the busyness of the birthing unit.

Sexual Intercourse: Sexual intercourse has been used in different cultures to stimulate contractions for centuries. There are mixed reports on the success, but it is suggested often enough to couples that I will mention it here.

- Semen contains prostaglandins, which are thought to stimulate contractions.

- Most care providers would not recommend having sex once the membranes are ruptured.

> I certainly don't recommend you tell the couple to have sex, or ask why they don't!

Nipple Stimulation: Stimulating the nipple causes the release of oxytocin and thus contractions. Women can often feel the uterus contract while breastfeeding. I doubt that you will hear about this from your DiL if she tries it.

- The nipple is stimulated by rolling or pulling on the nipple or by using a breast pump.

- This is controversial because there is little control of the amount of oxytocin released.

Castor Oil: What my mother and the ancient Greeks before her used to induce labor was castor oil. It is a vegetable oil with a horrible taste and consistency. Here are the facts about castor oil:

> **One friend told me,** "My daughter used castor oil at the advice of her doula. She did go into labor, but also had horrendous diarrhea and thought she might deliver in the car going to the hospital. While it worked with her first overdue pregnancy, it did nothing to bring on contractions with her second baby."

- About 4 tablespoons has been shown to increase contractions.

- To help make it palatable, it is usually mixed in orange juice.

- If it is going to work, it usually happens within a few hours, but it is unpredictable, as are the side effects.

  — Once ingested, nothing can be done to stop the effects, including potentially explosive laxative actions, with diarrhea along with birth.

  — It can leave the woman exhausted and dehydrated.

- Intestinal cramps can mimic labor contractions, making it harder to assess what is actually happening.

- It is not advisable to take it without medical advice and immediate access to care.

Activity: Some women will get a burst of energy and activity, start cleaning the house, or begin "nesting" before the baby is born. Some experts suggest that women try pelvic rocking, sit and bounce on large exercise balls, walk, or swim to "get things moving." Late pregnancy is no time to suggest that a woman start a new activity that she hadn't done before, and a very pregnant woman needs to be careful with her balance.

Herbal remedies: Raspberry leaf still seems to be popular; it is now available in capsules, which is likely more concentrated than the portion a person could drink. Chamomile tea is no longer recommended for pregnant women—neither are aloe, coltsfoot, juniper berry, pennyroyal, buckthorn bark, comfrey, Labrador tea, sassafras, duck root, lobelia, or senna leaf teas. Other herbal teas—citrus peel, linden flower, ginger, lemon balm, orange peel, and rose hip—are generally considered safe in moderation (two to three cups per day).

> With my first pregnancy, I drank raspberry leaf, homegrown peppermint, and chamomile tea for two months. As my due date approached, I walked and walked and walked to try to stimulate labor.
>
> After ten days—nothing. I ended up having my membranes stripped, an induction, and eventually a C-section.

Some women try evening primrose oil or black/blue cohosh, which are used for premenstrual or menopausal symptoms, to promote softening of the cervix and contractions, but there is no science to support their use, and a woman would be advised to ask her care provider about this.

WHAT ELSE TO EXPECT

There has been a fair amount of change to what happens in the birthing room. The Technology has improved, but overall there is relaxation in who can be there and how things are done. For instance, gone are the long sterile gowns and many units are no longer using masks.

Monitors

You may or may not have had an electronic fetal monitor used to assess your own babies. The look of the machines has changed a bit, but they are basically the same. Two straps are attached to a pregnant woman's abdomen—one picks up the baby's heart rate by ultrasound, and the other monitors the pressure of the contractions. There are now portable "telemetry or wireless" monitors that allow the woman to keep walking rather than forcing her to lie attached to the monitor itself.

Most, but not all, hospitals or birthing centers do a twenty- to thirty-minute fetal monitor assessment of the baby when the woman is admitted. If she is in preterm labor, is being induced, has had a previous C-section, or has medical problems, or if the baby has health issues, she will be monitored more closely and maybe continuously.

- If there are concerns about the heart rate or if it is hard to find, they will sometimes put on an internal monitor. This involves screwing a very small electrode into the scalp. This will give a more accurate reading. Wires attach the mother to the monitor. This can be very scary for the parents.

Intravenous/Medications

Many women who birth in a hospital will have an Intravenous (IV) inserted as labor progresses. This allows her to have fluids, but also to get medications.

- Usually a woman is given oxytocin (the same used to induce labor) to contract the uterus after birth of the baby and stimulate the placenta to be delivered.

  — If there is no IV, it can be injected into the thigh.

- Putting the baby to the breast right away can also stimulate a contraction to cause delivery of the placenta.

Enemas

The dreaded enema. It was very common for all women of our age to have endured a small "fleet" enema in early labor. Enemas are rarely, if ever, given to laboring women anymore. Consequently, some women have full bowels and can often have a large bowel movement while pushing or during the birth. The odor may be embarrassing for the woman, and should you be lucky enough to be in the birthing room, do not show any dissatisfaction, it can't be prevented.

> *I apologize to those women whom I gave 3H enemas (3H: high, hot, and a hell of a lot) years ago. These were an awful and unique form of torture, by which we put huge amounts of hot water into the laboring woman's colon. The abdominal space is already compromised by the baby's head.*

Shaving

Another area of great progress: We don't generally shave the perineal area anymore in labour.

- Many women come in with much or all of their pubic hair removed already. This may surprise you as you watch to see the baby being born; it did me the first time, but it is the norm (e.g., the Brazilian wax job).
    - This drastic method of hair removal has been linked to infection.

Nutrition

Most women are usually not hungry in active labor. We don't usually prevent her from eating in early labor unless she is at increased risk of having a C-section.

- Popsicles are still a popular choice in labor. It may be something you can offer to bring in and keep in a cooler, along with ginger ale or other clear fluid she enjoys.

Pushing

When you had your baby, you were likely told to push when the cervix was fully dilated (10 cm), whether you felt like it or not. Or maybe after panting for a half an hour before you were fully dilated, suddenly a team of people were yelling "Push...push...push" into your ears, which you did until you were blue in the face and had spotty red marks (petechiae) and bruises on your face the next day! The postpartum staff all congratulated you for pushing so well.

If it was your first baby, you likely were allowed to push for two hours at the very most. If you already had a baby, you would be allowed to push for an hour or so before some type of intervention (vacuum, forceps, or C-section), was used or an obstetrician was called in.

> *Women can now push for many hours with no medical interference, as long as baby and Mom are coping.*

These days:

- As long as the health of mother-to-be and her baby is good, pushing can wait until she feels the urge to bear down.

- She can even have a nap if her epidural is working!

- Then she can push leisurely for hours.

- Different positions may be suggested: upright, on all fours, or lying on her side, but for the most part, it is hands off.

Vacuum Extraction

If the mother has pushed and is exhausted, or if there is a problem with the baby's heart rate, the vacuum extractor may be used. This involves applying a cup to the baby's head and applying suction with a machine. Then a doctor or midwife guides the vacuum under controlled pressure while the woman is pushing.

- There are usually only three attempts to pull with the vacuum. If nothing happens, likely an obstetrician will be called to either apply forceps or do a C-section.

- The baby can have a cephalohematoma, a bruise that looks like a large swollen hickey, on the top of her head.

Forceps

There is a good chance that you were delivered with forceps. Your baby was less likely to be born that way, and your grandchild is unlikely to be born that way. However:

- We are seeing resurgence in the use of forceps, but not all care providers are experienced in their use.

- If the woman does not get an epidural, applying the forceps can be very uncomfortable.

- Babies can have marks and bruises on their face from the "blades" of the forceps.

Episiotomy and Tears

Most women who gave birth vaginally in the 1970s and 1980s had an episiotomy. It involves cutting through the perineum down from the vagina toward the anus or to the side. They were done to avoid the woman tearing, but sometimes they "extended" and the woman tore anyway.

Now women are more likely not to have an episiotomy. The birth of the baby is managed more slowly and carefully, and more time is given for the woman's perineal area to stretch and thin out. Women do sometimes have small tears that may or may not be sutured (sewn) up.

> Women with vaginal soreness or repairs are still encouraged to sit in the bathtub a few times a day and to pat dry, front to back. We don't use heat lamps anymore because they dry out the incision.
>
> *Ice is soothing and reduces swelling.*

A woman can have a small (first-degree) or a more serious third- or fourth-degree tear. A third-degree tear extends into the anal sphincter, and a fourth-degree tear goes into the rectal wall. A woman with a bad tear is likely to be uncomfortable, especially when sitting, going up and down stairs, or doing anything that puts strain on the area.

It will be especially important to help her with housework. If you were unlucky enough to have one of these tears, you may have sat on a red rubber ring, but use with caution as they can cause undue strain on the tear and increase swelling and pain. If she wants to try, she might try to keep her butt together as she sits on it. She can put a soft cushion over a ring, and some medical supply stores sell special soft rings.

C-Section

Although the rate varies across the globe, approximately 25 to 30 percent of babies are born by caesarean birth (C-section) in North America.

> The C-section mother needs help with childcare and housework for the first six weeks.

Urgent problems [e.g., problems with the baby, bleeding, lack of progress, or other complications such as first-time breech (feet/bum first) or the afterbirth (placenta) coming first] usually require a C-section birth. Many believe that the high rates of litigation in obstetrical practice have caused the C-section rates to increase.

- Most C-sections are done by spinal anesthetic unless there is an emergency that doesn't allow time for it to be done.
  - This limits the mother's movement immediately after the baby is born.
  - A woman will rarely be given a general anesthetic.

- C-section is major surgery, and she may have had a difficult, long labor too.

- Women usually go home on the third day unless there are complications.

- She needs to avoid heavy lifting, carrying nothing heavier than the baby for six weeks.

TOLAC/VBAC

> A woman may feel pressure to have a VBAC, but it is her decision to make with her doctor.

"Once a section, always a section" is not necessarily true. Now women with caesarean

83

sections often experience a TOLAC (trial of labor after Cesarean) or a VBAC (vaginal birth after Cesarean). Of those who try VBAC, sixty to eighty percent of women will go on to deliver a baby vaginally in future pregnancies.

- There is risk of ruptured uterine scar or other hemorrhage.
  - Therefore, the woman and the baby will be monitored more closely and kept from eating, in case she needs an immediate C-section.

Every woman, each labor, and every baby is different. You don't want a mother to feel like a failure or that she didn't try hard enough if she ends up with a C-section or having forceps used. Celebrate how hard she worked and the good outcome (that is, a healthy baby and mother) as the most important things to comment on. If the outcome is not good, assure her that she did everything that she could (See–When Things Don't Turn Out as Planned).

Pain Relief

While we might hope that all women and their babies can experience a natural childbirth, without any interventions or pain relief, giving birth is painful.

One most wonderful, gentle woman who has helped many women cope with childbirth is Penny Simkin. Penny is a physical therapist, doula, and expert in all things related to comforting the pregnant and laboring woman. She has given endless workshops and has books and videos available for anyone wanting to help a pregnant woman manage her pain (http://www.pennysimkin.com/).

> Keep your hand close to hold. Freshen facecloths with cold water.
>
> Support or fill in for her partner, however you can.

Epidural and Spinal Anesthesia/Analgesia

Many women have an epidural. It involves the injection of an analgesic (pain reliever) and/or a mild anesthetic (freezing agent) into the epidural space around the spinal column.

- Some ask for an epidural when they are admitted, but it is intended for those in established labour (3–4 cm. dilated and regular contractions.)

- Most physicians do not insert an epidural after 8 cm dilation, but some will try as long as they can.

Spinal anesthetic is injected directly into the space closest to the spinal column.

- The woman will be numb from about the nipple line down.

  — She will not be able to move her legs and will need a urinary catheter.

- She may have low blood pressure or a headache afterward.

Some hospitals offer a combined spinal/epidural also known as a "walking epidural."

- It provides rapid pain relief while allowing the woman to move around and push more effectively.

Laughing Gas or Nitrous Oxide

You may not have had this or heard of it except in the dentist office, but there is a good chance that your mother used nitrous oxide (N2O) or laughing gas. N_2O is a mixture of nitrogen and oxygen that the woman inhales by mask. It is very effective for short-term pain relief if the labor has progressed too far for an epidural or other form of pain relief to be used.

- Never, ever hold or let anyone else hold the mask over the woman's face for her.

- If she cannot hold the mask, she doesn't get the gas, and some other method of pain relief will be needed.

Other pain relief

Women may be offered a narcotic like Demerol, Fentanyl, or morphine by injection, likely into her IV.

- For women in early labour, it can let them relax and sleep, and they make wake up in active labour or in no labour.

Some women find acupressure helpful, and others have tried transcutaneous electrical nerve stimulation (TENS) to reduce labor pain.

SOMETHING DIFFERENT

I wasn't sure whether to include these practices, but they are happening, so I thought you would want to know about them.

Lotus Birth and Eating the Placenta

Lotus birth or umbilical nonseverance occurs when the cord is not clamped and cut, rather the placenta remains attached to the baby until the cord completely dries and falls off. This takes a few days, although I have heard it take a week or more. During this time, the placenta is open to the air to prevent smell, salted to dry it, or various herb/oils put on it. This is a resurgence of ancient practice.

Placentaphagia is eating the placenta. It can be put raw into a smoothie, dried/desiccated and put into capsules for the mother to ingest, or cooked and eaten (in a stew). Proponents say that we are the only mammals that do not eat our placenta, and they tout many health benefits, including less postpartum depression and bleeding, decreased fatigue, increased breast milk production, and an overall sense of wellness. Others are concerned that there may be toxins in the placenta that may prove harmful to the mother's health later on. Research is needed to either dispel or confirm these myths to reassure mothers or alert them to potential problems.

> Support your daughter and daughter-in-law in how they birth, recognize every labour is unique, and do not make them feel badly if you birthed much more easily than they do.

6. Taking Care of Mom

Some Things have Changed

Sixty years ago, women did not get out of bed or have a shower for the first week after giving birth. Thirty years ago, you probably had a sponge-bath the first day, even longer if you had a C-section. Now women who have vaginal births often shower in the birthing room and then go by wheelchair to their postpartum room, and are wearing their own clothes (rather than hospital gowns) later that day.

Most new mothers who deliver vaginally are in and out of the hospital within a day or so. This may be due to costs or bed shortages, but also the desire of women to be in their own homes with their own food and bed enjoying their new family without interruption. These short hospital stays make it more challenging for new parents and the nurses caring for them.

Conflicting Information from Staff

In all my years of nursing, the most common and frequent complaint from new mothers is that everyone tells them something different—nurses, doctors, and gulp, grandparents. Factor in all that they learned

> Knowing that the new parents may already be overwhelmed, think before you speak.

in pregnancy and you can imagine their overload. However, I also know new parents are never fully prepared for all there is to know about taking care of their first baby.

Many mothers are exhausted—not just by having a baby, but also by their stay in the hospital. When I have students in the postpartum unit, I encourage them to watch the extraordinary amount of traffic going in and out of the parents' room. All of this while the parents are trying to get to know and learn how to care for their baby, complete government forms, establish feeding, recover from delivery, and catch up on their sleep.

> Take your cue from the parents: if they are yawning or looking at each other, leave.

You may want to visit often and stay long; however, there are usually strict visiting hours for all but the identified support people. Depending on the time the baby is born and the delivery itself, visits can prove exhausting for the parents. Visits with everyone who might want to see the baby also cuts into the parents' time for learning how to care for the baby.

> You can be a door attendant, fielding unnecessary visitors, and unsolicited interruptions.

AT HOME

Because they go home so soon after the birth, it is very likely that the new mother (and the family) will need help, either, from you or someone else. If you live far away, aren't physically up to it, can't take time off work, or just aren't inclined, perhaps you can help by paying for a cleaning service or arrange for some help with shopping or a nursing home-support service.

> Recognizing the importance of support, in some cultures, women are cared for and learn to mother in special convalescent homes or by female relatives for up to months after they give birth.

When the public health nurse came to visit when my grandson was two weeks old, I answered the door. She called me by my daughter's name and, when I told her I was her mother, she was surprised that someone was there to help her. She said too many women are trying to manage at home alone in those first few weeks.

Don't Come Now...Why Aren't You Here?

More than a few grandmothers I know, especially those with children living in a different city, were told not to come immediately after the baby was born, but rather to wait for a week or two.

I am not sure where this message is coming from for these new parents for them to be alone, but in each case, the grandmother has gotten a call to come earlier and usually they are asked to stay longer than planned. It may not be feasible, but you might want to plan for flexibility around the time of the birth.

> **One new grandma said,** *"I was confused and hurt when my daughter told me not to come when the baby was born, to give them time to 'bond with the baby.' I just wanted to be there to help. Then two days later she was calling me, crying, but I had already made other plans. I did go as soon I could, but not as quickly as she wanted me there."*

THINGS TO WATCH

Postpartum is a time of fluctuating emotions and moods (See— Emotions). There are many normal physical changes in the first six weeks after giving birth. Postpartum women are more vulnerable to bladder infections, infection of episiotomy or C-section scar, constipation, hemorrhoids (from pressure or pushing), mastitis (breast infection), blood clots (complaints of pain in calves or shortness of breath), anemia (from blood loss), thyroid problems (hypo- or hyperthyroid), and hypertension. A significant concern is bleeding/hemorrhage.

Bleeding

Women are often surprised when they are told to get pads to wear after the birth, but they are necessary for the discharge as her uterus contracts and returns to

> *A friend's daughter, one week postpartum, mentioned to her that she had passed a clot in the toilet. Her mother was smart enough to ask about the size of the clot. It was huge (large grapefruit), with a steady flow of bright red blood. She took her to the hospital, towels soaking through. Her daughter had a month of many complications from the hemorrhage. Doctors told her she would have died without getting help so quickly.*

89

normal. In case you have forgotten, the bloody flow can last up to six weeks, but it is usually only bloody for the first few days, then pink and minimal after the first week, then yellow and white.

We have had women start hemorrhaging when camping or shopping in the first few weeks after giving birth. By the time they reach the hospital, they have lost a lot of blood, and need transfusions. We never want to give childbearing women blood products because we want to avoid possible antibody reactions in future pregnancies.

Here is the best way to avoid a hemorrhage:

- Encourage breastfeeding; it helps keep the uterus contracted.

- Be vigilant to anything unusual.

    — Any clot much larger than a silver dollar or twonie (two-dollar Canadian coin) may indicate that the uterus is not contracting well.

- If she is bleeding, make sure she empties her bladder, and get her to put the baby to her breast.

- If the bleeding does not stop, get her professional help.

- Tampons are not advised in the first six weeks after having a vaginal delivery.

> For any woman, at any time in her life,
>
> soaking one pad an hour with blood warrants a call to her doctor or visit to emergency clinic.

HOW TO HELP

Sometimes it is up to us to offer the help that they need. Here are some concrete ways to help and to spend time with your grandfamily.

Housework

One woman told me how her mother had traveled many thousands of miles to "help" after her first baby was born. She had hoped her mother would do laundry and make meals, as well as spend time with the baby. Instead, while she recovered from giving birth, struggled to find her way as a new parent, and maintain the household, her mother sat holding the baby for hours between breast feeds. When her mother returned home, she told the family how she was glad that she had helped with the new baby! Meanwhile, the new mother was exhausted and very happy to have only herself, her baby, and her husband to care for after she left. Now that she is becoming a grandmother, she is committed to helping in the ways she wished she had been.

> One of my daughter's friends was clear: *"Ask what you can do to help, particularly with a new, first-time, mom. Offer things that you are willing and able to do: make dinner, vacuum, do laundry, hold the baby at four a.m.. New moms are often so overwhelmed they don't know what they want or need you to do."*

While holding a sleeping newborn baby is one of life's most precious experiences for many of us, unless the baby is very fussy or cannot be put down for some other reason, it isn't necessarily helpful to the new mother to just sit and hold the baby while she is cooking your meals and doing housework. Let the mother have that pleasure with her newborn and you can have your cuddle time when the mother is showering, sleeping, or doing things that only she can do.

> A sweet new mother admitted, *"Even when my husband's mom would ask me, 'What can I do to help?' I would usually say, 'Nothing'. But if she said, 'Can I make stew for dinner tonight'? I would say, 'Absolutely. That would be great.'"*

One of the most successful grandmothers I know (successful in that she is a welcome and active part of her grandfamily's life) quietly helps her daughters-in-law with their housework. This behind-the-scenes grandparenting might not be glamorous or immediately recognized, but it makes a huge difference for the new family.

Your relationship with your child and his or her partner will determine how comfortable both of you are doing things in their home. Sometimes, you might feel in the way. To feel more comfortable, you might want to start helping before the baby is born. That way you can learn how they do things, where things go etc.. Be honest: "I want to help now so that I am better able to help you later."

I know that I didn't always put things away in the right spot, but I tried to do as many mundane tasks for my daughter and her husband as possible. With a new baby, likely no one is sleeping much. While they are napping or feeding the baby, you can quietly prepare meals, empty cat litter, take the dog for a walk, or do laundry. I was careful to ask if I could wash and put away my daughter's and her husband's laundry because it meant I would be going into their closets and drawers. They said that they were thankful for this, and I was happy to help.

Most of the grandmothers I spoke with said they just go ahead and do housework, but if you know that your daughter or daughter-in-law is very sensitive about you doing such things in her house, you can say, "I could fold the laundry for you."

> *Sometimes, just do what needs to be done. If the kitchen garbage is full, quietly empty it.*
>
> *If they get angry, don't do it again, but you have tried.*

If you think she might perceive this as your being critical of her, then just leave it be (and keep your mouth shut). Walk around the block, call your spouse or a friend, but keep your negative thoughts out of your relationship with her right now.

One grandmother I know has an amazing ability to stay in her son and daughter-in-law's very chaotic and somewhat disheveled house. I know I want to sweep the floors, and do the dishes when I am there for five minutes. But, somehow, when she visits from across the country, this wise, very well-coiffed grandmother fits into their lifestyle rather than trying to make it fit her values of homemaking. This seems to be a very happy family. The young children are clean, polite, and content. This wonderfully engaged grandmother visits often, always with a smile on her face, and hugs them as she arrives and leaves.

> *Encourage your spouse to help more at your house, since if you are helping at one house and then doing your own housework, you will quickly become exhausted.*
>
> **Pace and take care of yourself too!**

7. TAKING CARE OF BABY

Babycare is where you are likely going to see the most change. Most birthing units or hospitals do not have "newborn nurseries" anymore. "Rooming-in" with our baby meant that she went back to the nursery to be cared for by nurses at night, when we had a nap, and when we had visitors. Now, unless the mother or baby has a medical problem, chances are the baby will be cared for 24/7 by the parents in the mother's room.

While having the baby in the room all the time can help the new family bond or attach, it also means there is little time for the mother or her partner to rest. This can be a challenge if the mother is exhausted or has had a difficult birth or if there are problems with feeding the baby that require extra support from the nursing staff.

EARLY CARE

If babies are unstable at birth, premature, or have some other complication, they may be admitted to the Neonatal Intensive Care Unit (NICU). These units are often crowded with many babies, care providers, parents, and a lot of equipment. Most accommodate visits from siblings and grandparents, but because of the risk of infection and out of a desire for practicality, it is not always possible. You may have to be content with a picture and update. That's not to say you can't be in the waiting room to support the parents or in the mother's room if she is still in the hospital. Don't make things difficult for them if you aren't able to go in yet to see or touch the baby right away.

Skin to Skin

You may have heard of "skin to skin" and wondered what it means. The baby's clothes are removed, and usually only the diaper is left on. The baby is laid on the mother's naked chest, and both of them are covered with a warm blanket.

> If the baby is cold, the mother is encouraged to do skin-to-skin contact to increase the baby's temperature.
>
> *A baby who is cold will not feed well and can have low blood sugar.*

- Skin-to-skin warming can quickly increase the baby's temperature, but also to share the mother's microbes with the baby. It is advised for the breastfeeding and nonbreastfeeding baby.

  — Fathers and adoptive parents also do skin-to-skin.

- There is some evidence that babies benefit from skin-to-skin and the mother's normal skin flora (bacteria).

Some nurses are not comfortable with skin-to-skin contact and prefer to put the cold baby under a warming light or in an incubator. This can be done in the mother's room, although some may take the baby to another area on the unit.

Bath Time

I cringe to think of nurses who used fine scrubbing brushes and cold water to bathe newborns years ago. Now babies are dried off right after the birth with a towel, and that is usually all that happens until they have a bath later when their temperature stabilizes.

Consequently, the baby might still have "vernix" on her skin. This white, creamy substance is more

> *The baby might have some blood in her hair, but there is no need to comment or be concerned. She isn't being ignored; they are waiting until her temperature has stabilized to bathe her. This can take a few hours, but it also gives the new family uninterrupted time to get to know one another.*

common when the baby is preterm. It moisturizes the baby's skin and is thought to help lubricate babies during birth (although in full-term babies, the amount is minimal). It will slough off over time.

Many places no longer wait until the umbilical cord has fallen off to put babies in a little bathtub. We suggest bathing baby every few days to avoid drying the skin. Instead, the baby should have daily sponge baths for the first week or so. Babies can then be bathed daily if needed, but remember that babies have delicate skin that needs to be cleansed gently. Always pay special attention to the wrinkles, under the neck, in the groin, armpits, and between fingers and toes.

If you are lucky enough to be part of bathing your new grandbaby, have all of the things you need ready for the bath: clean clothes, diaper, towel, etc., and remember:

- The temperature of the baby needs to be above 98°F (Fahrenheit) or 36.7°C (Celsius).
  - The mother may use skin-to-skin contact or a lamp to heat the baby up before a bath.

- Regular soap can dry out baby's skin, increasing chances of infection.
  - There are lots of mild baby washing products available.
  - Bubble baths are discouraged until age three to avoid urinary tract irritation, especially in girls. There are some gentle ones the older child may use, but do not use your personal bubble bath; it likely will be too strong.

- Baby towels with built-in hoods will help keep baby warm and dry.
  - There are really cute ones that you can make or buy; they are much better quality than what we had for our babies.

- Many lotions are available to prevent skin chafing and drying, and it can calm baby to be massaged with oil or lotion.

> My grandson was born in early February, when the temperature can drop to -400C/0F.
>
> My daughter would pop a towel in the dryer to heat it up for her newborn after his bath.

- Keep the baby out of drafts and away from windows; a wet baby gets cold very quickly.

Cord Care

Most now leave the cord to air-dry, with no solutions, like alcohol or the purple dye, put on it.

> My friend's daughter phoned concerned that there was some bleeding when the cord fell off. As alarming as it may be, this is normal.

- Check for signs of infection (reddened skin, discharge); this is easy to do during diaper changes.
- The cord is left to fall off itself.

— This usually happens in the first two weeks, but it can take longer.

— If it doesn't fall off, some suggest putting alcohol on the stump, but avoid getting alcohol on the surrounding skin as it can break down.

Baby's Eyes and Vitamin K

These haven't changed much since your babies were born. Eye ointment is given, preventively, in case the mother has been exposed to a sexually transmitted infection that could lead to blindness in the baby.

> Unless the parents have discussed otherwise with their doctor, the baby will get eye ointment and Vitamin K soon after birth.

Your children likely had silver nitrate, which often left a black line or mark around the eyes. Now, unless the parents refuse, all babies get an antibiotic ointment in their eyes. This ointment does not leave any marks. I had the same ointment for my eyes a few years ago for dry eye; I was surprised how it stung and how blurry my vision was afterward. I completely understand why we don't want to put it into the baby's eyes when she is meeting her parents for the first time!

Vitamin K is essential for normal clotting of blood. It is produced by bacteria in food in the gut, but babies have not eaten yet and have only small amounts in their bodies.

- Vitamin K is injected into the big muscle of baby's thigh (with a very small needle), usually within the first few hours, but no later than six hours after birth.

- If the mother is in preterm labor, she may be given Vitamin K to try to prevent cerebral (brain) hemorrhage before the baby is born.

Tests

These haven't changed much since our babies were born. All babies have their heel pricked for blood to test for various problems such as PKU (phenylketonuria-a metabolic disorder that requires a special diet to avoid brain damage), cystic fibrosis, and thyroid levels within a few days after they are born. If not done at the hospital, the parents may have to take the baby to a laboratory. Some places repeat the tests a few weeks later. Many babies also routinely get a bilirubin test before they go home or from a public health nurse (See—Jaundice).

Most babies have their hearing checked in the hospital or in the first few weeks. Hearing loss might be caused by infection in the mother while she is pregnant or in the baby itself, or it can occur in babies that are born preterm. Less than one percent of babies have hearing problems, but such problems can lead to learning, social, and safety problems for the child.

Infant Nutrition

The WHO and major pediatric organizations encourage exclusive breastfeeding for the first six months, and ongoing breastfeeding for the first two years.

Infant feeding has changed—a lot. Women tend to follow their mother when it comes to feeding their babies. Even so, things have evolved in the last sixty years. You were likely formula fed if you were born in the fifties or early sixties. You were more likely to have breastfed your children in the seventies or eighties.

Research suggests, "Breast is Best" for babies and their mothers. Babies who are breastfed are less likely to end up in the hospital with gastrointestinal or respiratory infections. They have fewer allergies, less risk of Sudden Infant Death Syndrome (SIDS), and less obesity and diabetes, as they get older. Mothers who breastfeed return to their non-pregnant state more quickly, are less likely to have postpartum hemorrhages, and are at decreased risk of both breast and ovarian cancer later in life.

You will definitely have your own infant feeding stories. These will include either your success with breastfeeding if it worked for you, or your own trials and challenges if it did not. If you didn't try to breastfeed, you will have your own reasons for not doing so. If your daughter or daughter-in-law decides to breastfeed, this may be foreign to you, but she still needs your support for her choice. And, you need to know something about it so that you can help rather than alienate her.

> One friend told me, *"My mom came after both kids were born, which was good, but I am glad she didn't come in the first two weeks—she didn't breastfeed us, and would have encouraged me to quit breastfeeding."*

Here are some facts about breastfeeding today:

- New mothers need support as they learn to feed their babies.

- The WHO and major pediatric associations encourage women to breastfeed exclusively for the first six months.

  — Exclusive breastfeeding means that the baby gets nothing but breast milk, either directly by the mother's breast or pumped and given by bottle, syringe, or spoon.

- This doesn't mean the baby won't ever have a bottle; mothers can pump Expressed Breast Milk (EBM) to be put in bottles so the baby can be fed by others (including you!).

  > Our babies were likely on a three- to four-hour feeding schedule, but most newborns fed now "on demand," every two to three hours, with at least eight feeds in twenty-four hours.

  — The EBM goes into handy little pouches or bottles that attach to the pump; be sure all items are BPA-free (BPA is an environmental hormone that is released when polycarbonate baby bottles and other plastic containers are heated, washed in a dishwasher, or boiled).

> For the exclusively breastfed baby who needs expressed breastmilk, by bottle or tube, be aware that she may only need a few ounces at a time.

— The pouches can be sealed and are very convenient to go in the freezer and are defrosted slowly in a container of warm water.

• Babies can also be fed by spoon, or by a small tube taped to the breast or someone's finger (finger feeding).

Iron. Breastfed babies older than six months of age may need to be supplemented with iron until they are well established on solids (See–Solids).

• Iron can interfere with calcium absorption, so don't give iron supplement with milk or other calcium-rich foods.

Vitamin D. Breastfed babies need an additional 400 IU per day of Vitamin D.

• There is no need for additional Vitamin D for a formula-fed baby.

How long?

There has been much controversy about the length of breastfeeding. A 2012 *Time* magazine cover showed a four-year-old breastfeeding. This caused a huge outcry, but it also opened up the discussion. The WHO promotes breastfeeding until a child is two years of age, with ongoing benefits to immunity and attachment, and many cultures do breastfeed beyond this.

> One impassioned young mother of two told me, "Do not ask, 'When are you going to stop breastfeeding?' or 'Are you still breastfeeding?' This may cause her to be defensive and create unnecessary tension between you. It is not unnatural or improper to breastfeed past the infant stage or longer – you just might not be accustomed to it. If you stopped breastfeeding after a couple weeks or didn't even try, you likely think that formula feeding is best. But it isn't for us."

How long your daughter or daughter-in-law breastfeeds might not be determined until the baby is ready to wean. It may make you uncomfortable to see a pre-schooler breastfeed, but there is no known harm.

Breastfeeding Support

Most women need help to initiate and continue to breastfeed.

- Many communities have lactation consultants, and some doulas provide breastfeeding support.

- La Leche League (LLL) has been around for a long time. You may have contacted them or read their book (*The Womanly Art of Breastfeeding*), which was pretty much the only breastfeeding support for us. You might have also attended one of their groups. http://www.llli.org/.

- Now, there may be other local support groups, and there are many different blogs online. www.kellymom.com is particularly helpful with medical and social advice, with lists of local breastfeeding support centres.

Some health facilities offer breastfeeding classes. My son-in-law could not attend, so I went with my daughter. Very few men were there that night, and a few grandmothers came in their place. Encourage your son to attend all of the classes with his partner. Studies show that a supportive partner is one of the largest predictors for breastfeeding success.

Shortly after my grandson was born, I was fortunate to attend a "Breastfeeding Café" with my daughter and five-week-old grandson. This was a drop-in group for mothers wanting to talk about breastfeeding, and it was facilitated by a lactation consultant. I went with my daughter to help her with driving in the winter post C-section and for my own learning (as a new grandmother and a nurse).

> *Ask if you can go with them to prenatal classes when breast-feeding is on the agenda or to a special breastfeeding class if possible.*

There was another grandmother there, my age, also attending with her daughter and first grandson. We both had breastfed our children for over a year, each with no bottles, and agreed that somehow breastfeeding had become very complicated since we had our babies. Very little in life is simple anymore, and breastfeeding is no exception.

Nowadays, there is a gadget for absolutely everything, and breastfeeding, as natural as it should be, is no exception. One of the most annoying contraptions out there is the "hooter hider," a piece of cloth that covers the baby as she nurses from her mother's breast. There is usually a strap of some kind at the back that keeps it up over the mother's shoulder.

While many women love hooter hiders and feel comfortable, some babies do not breastfeed well while covered up. I think it's sad that nursing women are made to feel so uncomfortable when they feed their babies. Some women report getting many stares and unsolicited negative comments if they breastfeed without covering up, and for some even the sound of the baby nursing under the hooter hider has been enough for people to tell them to stop breastfeeding. While others say, they feel more conspicuous with a large cover up than if they just discretely lifted their shirt.

> One large breasted woman was perplexed, "Somehow, I breastfed my children while enjoying all the normal activities of life without feeling a need to hide my breasts, but women now seem to need to shroud their baby during breastfeeding."

Many women try to nurse, but not all of them breastfeed. There are a variety of reasons for this, including returning to work or school, hearing stories from their friends, their partner's discomfort, or if they have had breast reduction surgery they may not be able to lactate (produce milk).

Bottle, Formula, or Artificial-Baby-Milk Feeding

If the mother has tried to breastfeed without success, she may feel guilty and some talk about "failing" their baby. This is becoming quite common because breastfeeding is strongly encouraged and most women believe it is best for their baby, but they are not always

> Formula companies market artificial baby milk (ABM) aggressively. They claim ideal ratios of supplements for brain growth and baby health. As good as they try to make it; it is inferior to mother's milk.
>
> Still, we can be grateful that, when it is needed, formula is available.

supported to breastfeed. These mothers will need to use some type of artificial baby milk-formula.

For grandmothers, feeding the baby a bottle of formula or breast milk can be a wonderful thing because you get to hold and nurture the baby, but if you are going to feed the baby formula, then you need to know more:

- Babies need breast milk or proper infant formula until they are one-year-old. After that, they can have full-fat milk, which is necessary for nerve development.

> We no longer add cereal to the bottle to "help hold the baby" or to help her go to sleep.
>
> This was my mother's favorite suggestion for my exclusively breastfed children. If she heard them make a peep when I was talking to her on the phone she would say, "Poor thing must be hungry." She lived far away, so it wasn't a daily battle, but it was certainly annoying.

- There are many different kinds of formula using cow, goat, or soya milk.

- Evaporated milk, almond and rice milk and skim cow's milk lack adequate iron, protein, and fat for baby growth and development.

- Formula is slower to digest than breastmilk, so formula-fed babies generally eat less often. Young babies don't eat more than three or 4 ounces, or 90 to 120 ml, of formula, but as your grandchild grows, this will increase to 8 or 9 ounces (240–270 ml).

  — You need to know how much formula the baby has been eating so that you don't under- or overfeed her.

- The parents need to talk to their care provider to determine the best type of formula for the baby.

- Formula is expensive

  — The new family might appreciate it if you buy the occasional case of the formula they use.

- Formula comes in three ways: as a powder to mix with water, in concentrated liquid, or in ready-to-serve cans.

  — Check and follow instructions.

- There are many different bottling systems, but whatever is chosen needs to be BPA-free.

- Hopefully, there will be a supply of bottles with formula for you to use.

  — They can be prepared and stored for up to twenty-four hours.

  — If the bottle is left out for longer than an hour or so, throw the contents out.

- There are bottle warmers to warm formula kept in the fridge, or you can put a bottle in a container of hot water.

  > *Never, ever heat formula, breast milk, or any other food meant for baby in the microwave.*

  — Babies have had severe burns to their mouth and esophagus from people wanting to rush-heat formula or other foods in the microwave. Formula and food continues to "cook" and get hot after they come out of the microwave.

- Bottles come with different air-vent systems, and some are angled to help prevent the baby from swallowing too much air.

  — Despite all these fancy gadgets, babies, including breastfed ones, still need to be burped. However, you may find that a breastfed baby does not burp or spit up as much as a formula-fed baby.

Sterilizing bottles and nipples by boiling everything in saucepans of water works, but it has been revolutionized with the invention of the microwave! You will be impressed:

- Clean bottles, nipples, and soothers can now be put in special, reusable pouches with a small amount of water and are then microwaved to steam-sterilize for short periods.

- Be careful when you open them because they build up a lot of steam.

Pacifiers

Pacifier, soother, binkie...whatever your family calls them, their use remains as contentious as ever. My mother told me how my grandmother would put a soother in my mouth whenever she visited, and she would throw it into the fire after my grandmother left.

A lot of us tended not to use pacifiers. In my group of friends, it would have been perceived as not attending to your baby. I know I didn't use them with my children, but my grandson used one for about a year at naptime or when he was teething. Then he threw it away

> It is not worth an argument your child over pacifier use.

when he no longer wanted to use it—he even chucked them through the cat door!

There is a lot to know about pacifiers today:

- Today's pacifiers come in many different varieties, shapes, and sizes.

- They are suggested for sleep only.

- Pacifiers need to be sterilized regularly in the same way as bottles.

- There can be an increased risk of otitis media (middle ear infection) and teeth problems with excessive soother use.

- Some people worry that pacifier use causes "nipple confusion" and is detrimental to breastfeeding.

  - I haven't noticed this. Some babies just like to suck, and the mother has to be able to detach from the baby once in a while.

> Pacifiers provide "non-nutritive sucking," which is sucking for the sake of sucking.
>
> Pacifiers can soothe a fussy baby and help decrease the risk of SIDS.

- Some specialists believe that prolonged pacifier use leads to speech delays and lisps and is harmful to teeth development.
  — There are "orthodontic" pacifiers on the market for those worried about this, but I am unsure of their effectiveness.

- It's best not to use pacifiers after twelve months of age
  — Due to decreased risk of SIDS after that time and increased risk of ear infection with ongoing pacifier use.

- There are clips to attach the soother to the baby (no pins or strings needed anymore).

Solids

Introducing solid foods into a baby's diet has changed drastically in the order and way they are given. We didn't let our babies enjoy regular adult foods because we didn't want to give them a "sweet tooth" or cause allergies; consequently, baby often had a separate menu and mealtime with lots of little prepared jars (handy for buttons or paints later) or we hand-pureed cooked vegetables and fruits. Some people still try to force sloppy food into the dawdling baby before they can literally get their tongue around what they are eating.

Pediatricians and allergists encourage parents to let their children enjoy a variety of foods after six months of age; some will allow small rice cereal as early as four months, as it is very easy for babies to digest, but most honour the WHO guidelines for exclusive breastfeeding for the first six months.

> **Follow the parent's method of feeding their baby**
>
> **One mother of one was still angry when she told me,** *"My mother annoyed me to no end by constantly trying to slip my son a spoonful of ice cream or piece of chocolate.*
>
> *Not only were these 'special treats' not good for him, they also undermined us as his parents."*

Readiness to Eat

The American Academy of Pediatrics (AAP), the Canadian Paediatric Society, and Health Canada sug-
gest waiting until babies are six months old before introducing solids. By then baby should have achieved these physical milestones:

> *Even if the baby is able to feed herself, never leave her unattended.*

- Able to sit with support, good head and neck control.

- Push up with straight elbows from lying face down.

- Show readiness for food by putting her hands or toys in her mouth.

- Able to swallow when food is put in her mouth

- Leaning forward and opening her mouth when interested in food, and turning away when uninterested in the food or not hungry.

Food to Eat

Baby's iron stores diminish after about 6 months and their rapid growth increases need; therefore, experts advise to start with the iron and zinc rich foods such as meat, eggs, and iron-fortified cereals. Foods are introduced one at a time, waiting two to three days before starting another. After each new food, parents are told watch for any allergic reactions, for example diarrhea, rash, or vomiting.

> **Babies and toddlers have needs for high iron.**
>
> *After six months of exclusive breastmilk or formula, try baby with ground meat, eggs, and iron enriched cereals.*

Breastfeeding (or iron-rich artificial baby milk formula) should continue to be the main source of nutrition until they are one-year-old. Feeding only cow's milk in the first year will leave her nutritionally deprived because, while it is a good source of calcium and Vitamin D, it is not a good source of iron. When they can drink cow's milk at one year, it should be whole fat (homogenized).

Once iron-rich foods are successfully introduced, other solids are given including sweet potato, rice, corn, squished peas (to prevent choking and increase ability to get nutrients from them. Homemade soup can be a messy, but healthy option. Small muffins can include sweet potato and other foods.

> I like to make soup. At a young age, my grandson would say "mmm" with each spoon full. When he really likes it, especially, chicken soup, he will pick up the bowl to drink the liquid more quickly. I can easily add chopped spinach and other high-iron foods into the soup.

Some foods are delayed until the baby is one year of age, and others should be avoided for even longer:

- Honey can contain botulism spores, and a baby's stomach is not acidic enough to destroy them.

- Whole nuts are a choking hazard for babies and toddlers.

- Peanut butter can be a choking hazard for children under two. If given, should be spread thinly, not given as a spoonful.
  - If there is a family history of severe nut or peanut allergy, it is recommended that the parents ask their doctor about doing an oral food challenge before introducing peanut or other nut butters into the baby's diet.

- Popcorn is not recommended for children under age four.

- Babies should not be offered sugary drinks or foods (such as candies, soda pop, or energy drinks).

- Home-prepared spinach, beets, green beans, squash, and carrots are avoided in young babies as they may contain large amounts of nitrates (commercial baby food tests for nitrates so may be safer).

Feeding babies does not require a lot of equipment or separate food purchases. Mothers can use their blenders, ice cube trays with creative veggie and fruit concoctions, and iron-fortified infant cereals that come in single packages for ease of use. Babies are offered a much wider variety of foods now and they appear to enjoy it.

My daughter is a dietitian and suggests we vary foods offered. Remember to include iron, zinc, and protein-containing foods to toddlers, such as scrambled or hardboiled eggs, pieces of meat, or mini-sandwiches made with hummus (pureed chickpeas).

> My grandson likes to help me make hummus. We put a can of drained organic chickpeas, some olive oil, lemon juice, and sometimes parsley, chili powder, carrots, or sundried tomatoes in the blender. He is more eager to eat something he made.

You can also try tuna, meat, or nut-butters thinly-spread on toast can be placed in a muffin tin for a toddler friendly snack or meal.

Instead of only offering pureed foods, most babies now get "finger foods" that they feed themselves and therefore self-regulate their intake. Baby just needs to be able to hold larger pieces of food until she has mastered the pincer grip and can pick up smaller pieces (See–Choking or Gagging).

With the rise of childhood obesity, it is important to fol-

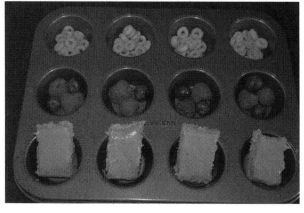

low the baby's own hunger cues. Babies are no longer force-fed. Well no one could force my grandson to eat anyway, even at an early age; he would just turn his head and hurl the spoon.

The trend towards infant-self feeding whole foods versus spoon-feeding purees may surprise you or make you feel uncomfortable. It did me. Do not make this a source of conflict with the baby's parents. Rest assured that new research supports this style of feeding.

My grandson is encouraged to explore his food at length and eat as he chooses from a variety of healthy foods. He ate very few prepared baby food items; while his appetite was not huge in the first year, it grew along with him. Because he ate regular adult food, we haven't found it hard to feed him at our house and he is comfortable trying new foods. Chicken curry was one of his early favourite dishes!

Baby or Infant-Led Weaning

Promotion of infant self-feeding at an early age is occurring at the same time as the emerging trend for parents to adopt this style of food delivery. More and more babies now experience the feeding trend of "baby-or infant led weaning" (BLW). Weaning may make you think of stopping breastfeeding or bottles, but with BLW, ending breastfeeding is not the goal; babies still nurse or use bottles once solids are introduced.

BLW, also called "baby self-feeding", refers to letting the baby eat like a regular member of the family with normal food when she is ready. BLW advocates suggest not using baby dishes for fear that baby hurl them across the room. My children were more likely to wear them on their heads, with uneaten food still on the bottom. The food is put right on the high-chair tray, which usually has a removable top layer.

> When I first heard about BLW, I was concerned about feeding adult food to babies, especially exposure to allergens and choking. I was reminded that children have been eating toast at an early age for many years, and contains a variety of ingredients that previously were a sensitivity worry.
>
> *Choking has not been a worry with my grandson; even without teeth, his gums were able to mash cheese, soft fruit, and cooked vegetables. If he couldn't 'chew' it, he would spit it out.*

When the BLW baby comes to visit, you are well advised to put a drop cloth on the floor because self-feeding can be a very messy way of eating. Mine is an old plastic tablecloth. Your pets will be very happy to see the baby come for a meal because they will get many treats that drop from the table!

Most surprising to me about BLW was seeing babies gnaw on meat bones—yes, you heard it right. If your granddaughter is teething, give her a T-bone! It makes sense. As long as the bone is not too soft and does not have shards, it can offer nutritional value and a handy object to teeth on while the family is eating.

Prepared Foods

While it is easy to feed a baby normal food, there is no shortage of prepared foods for babies of all ages. They come in creative and enticing packaging and gourmet-named varieties; buy baby a squishy tube of mango roasted corn risotto or black cherry yogurt rice and you may be tempted to try some yourself! Read the ingredients on the packages to make sure that the prepared foods you purchase do not contain excess salt and sugar.

Organic is very popular, but having tried a few of these cookie/ crackers at my son's playgroup, I

> In my local grocery, the side of one aisle is devoted to these products and a family could spend much of their food budget in the baby food section.

understand why baby might not be interested-ugh. There are also expensive, but convenient junior versions of almost everything.

Allergies

The best thing to do to help prevent allergies in your grandchild is to support your grandfamily's efforts to breastfeed. Some used to believe that a breastfeeding mother who avoids contact with allergens will lessen the chances of the child having a reaction to particular foods, such as milk and wheat, preferring to give only soy and rice, but the AAP disagrees.

> According to the Centers for Disease Control, about 4 percent of children under the age of 18 have food allergies. The following foods account for 90% of food allergies:
>
> 1. Cow's milk
> 2. Eggs
> 3. Peanuts
> 4. Tree nuts (walnuts, pecans, almonds, and cashews)
> 5. Fish
> 6. Shellfish
> 7. Soybeans
> 8. Wheat

Experts now advise that delaying the introduction of certain foods, such as eggs at one year, as we did, does not prevent allergies, especially if the baby is also breastfed. Rather, they believe that postponing exposure to these foods may actually *cause* allergies.

The rate of food allergies has increased over the past twenty years, perhaps because of the strict guidelines that most of us followed. It will be interesting to see if this trend changes with the new, more hassle-free approach.

Your child might speak to the baby's physician if there are concerns about a family history of allergies.

Gluten Sensitivity and Celiac Disease

Gluten and wheat sensitivity is a hot topic for many adults. We started our babies on rice cereal first because it was supposed to be easiest on their guts, and then we gradually expanded their diet to include grains. Many grains contain gluten.

- Breastfeeding appears to help protect babies from developing gluten sensitivity later in life.

- Gluten-containing products are introduced around six months of age, just as other foods are.

Beverages

The first time I heard my friend's two-and-a-half-year-old grandson ask for water instead of juice was a huge shock for me; my grandson was still exclusively breastfeeding so this was brand new to me.

Water, yes, water, likely in a "sippy cup."

- The AAP recommends water for babies over six months of age and to limit juice to 120ml (~1/2 cup) per day. Dilute it if baby is thirsty.

- Your grandchild can drink whole cow's milk when she is a year old. No more than 3 cup servings of milk should be given a day (if toddlers are consuming too much milk, they

Before he could talk, my grandson would get a cup from a kitchen drawer that contains his dishes, cutlery, and snacks, take my hand, and walk to the waterspout in the refrigerator for me to fill it. He has diluted juice after his nap, but now, much to my surprise, he asks for water.

may not have room for iron-rich foods. Also, too much milk may constipate baby).

- There is a large variety of sippy cups with different shapes, colors, and systems at the top, from a shaped mouthpiece to a straw. I bought one to have at my house. It has a screw top with a soft, durable straw that comes up through a hole at the top.

- The cup can be insulated or a lighter plastic but must not contain BPA.

- It is important for the baby's development to offer an open cup (use a bib!) and start with water.

Babies ought never to be put to bed with a bottle or sippy cup of juice or even milk because of the effects of sugar on the tooth enamel.

> I have seen toddlers who have consumed excess sugary drinks need an anesthetic to have their cavity-decayed baby teeth removed.

COMMON ISSUES

Cradle Cap

Despite new, specialized baby products, babies still get cradle cap. Cradle cap is crusty yellow patches of dry skin on the scalp and around the ears. It is self-limiting, usually clearing by the age of three months. We don't know what causes it– maybe maternal hormones, immature sebaceous glands, or a fungal infection, but not from poor hygiene. Babies with prolonged or severe cradle cap may be more likely to develop eczema later in life.

Parents will want to get rid of it, and usually wanting suggestions, here are tips you can pass along:

- Remember, scrubbing any skin or scalp area can break down the skin and leave the baby vulnerable to infection.

- Don't over-wash, it will dry out the scalp and increase the flaking.

- Olive or coconut oil massaged into the scalp can soften the patches, and then be very gently combed out.

- Some doctors suggest using anti-dandruff shampoo a few times a week, but avoid baby's eyes.

- The doctor may prescribe antifungal medications, for use only if fungal infection is confirmed.

- If the condition is severe or extends beyond the scalp, the doctor may prescribe a mild hydrocortisone cream.

Colic and Gas

I am so thankful that neither my babies had serious colic—just the occasional gassy time. If your grandbaby struggles with colic, it can be a difficult time for her and her parents.

Colic is incessant crying, usually with the legs drawn up to the abdomen, often in the evening in up to a quarter of babies. We don't know what causes colic, but some believe it is an immature gut or rarely intolerance to milk products (even ingested by the breastfeeding baby).

> I have burped many babies and have shown many parents how to, but when baby has colic, burping isn't going to fix the problem.

The mother can try a week or two trial of cutting diary from her diet and the formula fed baby can be offered soy or other formulas to see if that makes a difference.

Colic typically starts after the first few weeks and ends at around three or four months, but it can go on for a year. Breastfeeding appears to offer some protection from colic.

- The options for colic are pretty much the same as we had for our babies:

- Always burp the baby well.

- A swaddled baby is very easy to hold upright on your lap, pat her firmly on the back or you can lay the baby on her stomach with her head to the side and pat her on the back.

- Over the shoulder is a popular position that you likely used, and one friend said she walked her baby for hours every night for a year.

- Some mothers (and Dr. Sears) report that wearing their baby in a sling and walking the halls of their house helps. Others go out in stroller or in the car.

- Some promote eliminating dairy and other potentially irritating foods such as eggs, wheat, soy from the mother's diet, but there are conflicting reports, we need more research to know for certain.

  — Until then mothers can try to remove foods one at a time to determine the effect in her baby; if it helps then perhaps, she should keep it out of her diet.

- Gripe water and Ovol, which you may have used with your babies, are still around, but I can find no studies that show they work.

  — The original gripe water contained alcohol, often gin, but it is now usually a combination of various non-medicinal products such as bicarbonate soda, chamomile, and fennel.

    Check the label carefully, some gripe waters contain alcohol.

  — Chamomile tea is an "old-wives remedy". While there is no proof it works, there are no reports of harm and it can be psychological comforting for a parent to be able to do *something* in such a powerless situation!

- There are studies testing probiotics; they are already available at some pharmacies. One study has shown promising effects, but we need more research to recommend it.

- If you had a successful remedy, you may want to offer it to the new parents, but check first with CDC, Motherisk, or other health safety/baby organizations to ensure that it is approved for use.

- Although these products seem harmless, it may be best for the parents to discuss ongoing or serious colic with their physician to ensure that there is no underlying cause, such as reflux or an illness.

Circumcision

There is a good chance that your husband is circumcised. There is a lesser chance that your son or son-in-law is circumcised. Until the late 1970s, most baby boys were circumcised, especially if their father or siblings were. Today most boys are not circumcised unless the baby has an unusually tight foreskin that interferes with urination (called "phimosis") or for religious or cultural reasons.

> After thirteen years of recommending no circumcision, the AAP reversed their opinion in 2012 and now support the procedure.
>
> *This kind of switch in information can be very troubling to parents, who may now feel guilty or worry that they have to circumcise an older boy.* They don't.

After thirteen years of recommending no circumcision, the AAP reversed their opinion in 2012 and now support the procedure. This kind of switch in information can be very troubling to parents, who may now feel guilty or worry that they have to circumcise an older boy.

Parents can be assured that they do not need to circumcise a boy who is not having difficulties. The Canadian Pediatric Society is reviewing its stand on circumcision, reportedly to be neutral about the procedure, respecting the family's culture.

- Circumcision is usually done in the doctor's office.

- Unless medically indicated, most doctors will charge a fee.

For the uncircumcised baby, do not retract the foreskin during changes or baths.

- It will grow as the child does, and the doctor will check during routine medical exams.

- Swishing water around the genital area during the baby's bath is usually sufficient for cleanliness of the foreskin in the normal newborn.

- It is normal to have white smegma build up a little under the foreskin. If there is no redness or swelling, there is usually no reason for concern.

- Most boys will be able to retract their foreskins by five years of age. If after that you are concerned that the foreskin is too tight, you can encourage the parents to talk to their doctor.

Some cultures circumcise girls, also called female genital mutilation or cutting, it involves removal of all or part of the external female genitalia. You likely don't have to worry about this you unless one of your grandchildren's families belongs to one of the cultural groups that practice it (e.g., western, eastern, and northeastern Africa, in parts of the Middle East, and among some immigrants in Europe, North America, and South Asia). Many countries consider it a crime. Female circumcision is associated with ongoing medical and gynecological problems for the girl as she grows.

Jaundice

If your babies were jaundiced, it's more likely that your grandchildren will be, too. Around sixty percent of newborn babies become jaundiced, which means that the baby has yellow skin and yellowness in the whites of her eyes. Newborn jaundice is caused by a build-up of bilirubin, which is created when the red blood cells are broken down and the baby's immature liver. This usually clears up within a few weeks, but for some with breastfeeding jaundice or illness it persists for much longer.

Babies with high levels of bilirubin can be sleepier and have problems eating. If the bilirubin levels continue to increase without treatment and the baby is very jaundiced, there is a concern that the baby can get kernicterus.

> Because of some recent cases of kernicterus in untreated babies, many doctors are aggressive about treating jaundice.
>
> *Bilirubin levels are monitored by a blood test or a device that measures the bilirubin through the skin.*

Kernicterus is very rare. It happens when the high levels of bilirubin lead to deposits in the brain and other tissue and can lead to brain damage and deafness.

The treatment for jaundice is still the same as with our babies. They are exposed to bright light to break down the bilirubin in the skin and the body gets rid of it through urine and bowel movements. While under the light, babies only wear a diaper to reveal as much skin as possible and put in an incubator to avoid drafts. Baby will have patches over her eyes to avoid retinal damage. Now, there are also special biliblankets that provide the light directly to the skin. They make taking care of the baby much easier and some places will rent them for home use.

Teething

Teething hasn't changed. Babies still struggle and so do their parents, but, as expected, there are a few more gadgets to ease the pain.

> Be careful: Some teething gels contain a mild anesthetic (e.g., benzocaine) that can affect the swallow reflex and leave baby vulnerable to choking.

- Orajel is still available. (I sure used it for my babies and myself at times over the years.)

  — There are a few different brands and special varieties of tooth-pain gels now.

- Mesh soothers that can be filled with banana or placed in an ice tray with breast milk and frozen can provide good relief and are not known to cause choking. I found them to be quite large, and my grandson didn't use them much.

> While frozen teething rings can provide relief, and while giving a baby a piece of ice might seem cheap and convenient, it poses a significant choking risk and is an absolute no-no.

117

Teething Necklaces

Of all the things that are new to me, the teething necklace was one of the most frightening. The necklaces can be made from cotton, but most often, they are made out of amber or hazelwood stones. Amber contains succinic acid, which has analgesic properties when ground up or heated by the baby's skin. Critics point out that for succinic acid to be released the amber needs to be in extreme heat, such as in a fire. Perhaps it is the mother who is most soothed by the necklace, as she may be encouraged by the thought that she is doing something to help her baby.

Although they are called "necklaces" and I have seen babies wearing them around the neck, those who sell them protect their interests by advising that they are used only when the mother is holding the baby and

> Safety organizations suggest not to use teething necklaces.
>
> *If your grandbaby is using one, then you might have no influence, but please don't gift one.*

the baby is holding the necklace. Most have a break-away clasp, and the pieces of amber are supposed to be so small that they cannot cause a choking hazard! Some mothers wear them so that babies can teeth while they are holding them. Safety organizations advocate not using the necklaces at all.

ELIMINATION—DIAPERS.

The first few poops that the baby will have are called "meconium." This is dark green, tarry, and difficult to remove from the baby's bottom. You may not have seen meconium if your baby was put in the nursery, but now the

> *For those of you who may remember the stench of a formula-fed baby's poop, you may be surprised to find out that exclusively breastfed babies have somewhat sweet smelling or odourless poop.*

new parents have to deal with it! The earlier babies have this first poop, the less likely they are to be jaundiced. Early breastfeeding seems to help the baby get rid of the meconium sooner.

If you didn't breastfeed, you may not have experienced the often mustard-yellow colored, seedy poops that breast milk usually produces, although it may be brown at times. Some breastfed babies rarely poop, while others (like my children and my grandchild) pooped at least once (and often more) per feed in the early days. As solids are introduced or if baby has artificial baby, the poop becomes more formed, brown, and smelly.

Diaper Free!

Amazingly, some parents use no diapers at all. The premise of "Elimination Communication", infant potty training, and baby-led toileting, is that if the parents are aware of the baby's signals, they can determine if the baby will eliminate and sit them on a potty. Whilst this isn't widespread (yet), I have heard of mothers who start sitting babies on their potty after meals as young as three months old.

I was surprised in China to see toddlers walking around with their crotch wide open to the elements, no diaper of any kind. If they have to eliminate, they just seemed to crouch down when the need arises. I am not sure what happened before they were walking.

For the majority of parents, diaper purchases and changes are a necessary and great expense of having a baby. It appears that babies are in diapers longer than ever before. Apparently most children in 1957 were toilet-trained by eighteen months (that would be me), and most of our children were likely toilet-trained by age two, but now more and more children are not toilet-trained until they are three or four (See–Potty Training).

> The improvements in diapers and pull-up diapers may be contributing to the increased length of time to potty train.
>
> If baby does not feel wet and isn't uncomfortable in a soiled diaper, she may not as motivated to use the potty.
>
> Some disposable underpants have a cold-sensation to alert baby to the wet.

Cloth Diapers

Cloth diapers have made a comeback. They have really changed and for the better! Debate continues about the cost of detergent, the diapers, water, and energy efficiencies of diapering over a baby's lifetime versus using thousands of disposables. In some cities, diaper services pick up and deliver if the parents have neither the time nor inclination to wash the diapers themselves.

Diapering Systems

Cloth diapers now come in delightfully bold colors and designs. I was very impressed with the system my daughter chose, although they are all similar. The diaper is very flexible in fitting, with most claiming to be "one size fits all," with very few leaks, and my grandson had a very clear bottom! One quilting group here recently had a class to learn how to make the new diaper.

> You have to watch diaper cream. If, like my daughter, your child uses both methods of diapering—cloth at home and disposables for going out at night—it is very easy to use the wrong cream with the wrong diaper!

- There is an outer shell made from a non-porous but also non-rubberized/plasticized material.

  — There is a pad of material that fits into the little snap-on, cloth-like, diaper shell. There are no pins! No plastic pants. What a wonderful invention this is!

- The diaper pad might be made of hemp, bamboo, wool, or organic cotton.

- They have reusable liners made from wicking material so the baby stays dry.

- The parents need to use special detergents to ensure that the diapers remain absorbent.

- There are also special diaper creams available through the manufacturers of the cloth systems. Pure coconut oil is also safe.

  — Regular diaper creams made with petroleum, oil, or zinc create a barrier on the cloth diapers (especially diapers with synthetic fabrics or liners made of fleece) and will make the diaper repel rather than absorb and leak, rendering the system useless as it was designed.

- There are also adorable swimming versions of the shells.

- If you end up in the position of washing the cloth diapers, ensure you use the correct detergent and it is advisable not to dry the diapers if they use dryer sheets (they can leave residue in the machine that will cause the diapers to be both repellent and irritating to your grandchild's skin).

  — Dryer balls are a great alternative to dryer sheets; my grandson loves to put them in while helping with laundry.

- There is no need to rinse diapers of exclusively breastfed babies before putting in the washing machine. However, for formula-fed babies and babies who are eating solids, you will want to rinse out soiled diapers first.

> *Avoid flushing poop off diaper in the toilet as you may have. It is very tempting; but plumbers are more expensive and harder to get now!*

Disposable Diapers

Disposable diapers now fit much better and rarely leak, ball up, or shred. The nighttime diapers are especially absorbent. If you opened the original disposable diapers, you had to tape them shut.

> *Some disposables have gel that combines with the urine to keep the baby's skin dry.*
>
> *It is very easy to tell if the diaper is wet by feeling the different texture of the diaper gel, or with some, by seeing the little stripe on some of them change color.*

Most now have Velcro that you can open and shut as often as you like.

Disposing of the new diapers has also come a long way. When my daughter said she was going to buy a Diaper Genie®, I had no idea what she was talking about. When I realized it was essentially an expensive diaper garbage can, I suggested she just use a covered trashcan with plastic bags for liners. She knew better, the room doesn't smell at all, even after the most soiled diaper. Like many of her friends, she ended up with two because she wanted to have them wherever the baby was being changed often.

The diaper genie is a two-plus-foot plastic cylinder with a foot pedal that opens the top for you to put the soiled diaper in. When the genie won't let you put anymore diapers in the top, the fun really starts:

- You need to push a button to open the center of the genie. Inside you will find a long line of diapers in a plastic sheath. You have to cut the top of the sheath (the cutter is inside the cylinder) and tie a knot in the top.
  - Voilà, diapers are all wrapped like a big long blue sausage, ready for the garbage.

- Now you have to prepare another sheath for the next bunch of diapers.

- A blue round capsule goes into the top with the new sheath.
  - Fortunately, the round capsule has always had more sheaths ready for me.

- Then you need to tie a knot in the end of the new sheath that will emerge from the top of the genie.

If you are confused, rest assured, we all found this gadget mindboggling at first. Once mastered, it all makes perfect sense, and the system really is quite marvelous. Refills are costly so don't put in regular garbage. Changing the sheath is quite the production, and one you might want to attempt in private!

There are "swimmers," disposable diapers for the water. Pools require them.

As I learned this morning, not to inadvertently use regular disposables at toddler swim class as they absorb far too much water!

Diaper Rash

My grandson had an amazingly rash-free bottom until he was two and ate too many cherry tomatoes! Even while teething, I didn't see more than a bit of redness after a big poop. When he is in cloth diapers, he gets special, quite expensive creams. When he wears disposables, he gets nothing except for some zinc-based diaper cream if there is any sign of irritation.

Newborns usually get a protective layer of plain petroleum jelly on a cleaned, dried bottom to make it easy to remove the meconium poops of their first few days. If you are there when the nurses diaper the baby, you may notice that some of them have an odd habit of slathering the diaper with petroleum jelly rather than putting it directly on the baby's skin. I caution my students and to parents who may be tempted to copy them that this causes urine and stool (poop) to be captured between the diaper and skin and cause problems rather than protect the skin from the excretions that are meant to be absorbed by the diaper!

Instead:

- Make sure the baby's skin is completely clean.

- Use the petroleum jelly or a lanolin-based protective ointment on cleaned skin. Some babies might have an allergic reaction to lanolin, especially if either of the parents has a wool allergy.

    — As long as the baby has no irritation or diaper rash, petroleum jelly should work well.

- You may have used "A&D" ointment; it is still on the market.

- If the baby has a rash, parents can try to switch to disposable diapers for a few days and use a zinc-based ointment.

    — There are many special balms.

    — If this doesn't work, try olive oil or baking soda and warm water.

    — There are also colloidal oatmeal baths or baby ointments containing oatmeal.

- Some people advise using expressed breast milk on diaper rashes (as well as on all kinds of other baby cuts, burns, or infections).

- Avoid baby powder or other talcum powders because they can stick to the rash.

- "Diaper-free" time also can help.
    — Place naked baby on a waterproof changing pad on the floor, if you had daughters, remember to cover your grandson's lower body!

Baby Powder

While it can smell wonderful and elicit romantic notions of sweet little babies, the days of using baby powder are long over. Baby Power is one of those products (like bumper pads) that you have to wonder why it is still sold!

- Pediatricians advise against using talcum powder because inhaling the powder can cause serious damage to baby's lungs.

> One new mother reported frustration when grandma wanted to powder-up the new baby so that he *"smelled like a baby"*; her response was, *"But he already smells like a baby!"*

- It seems that some people still use cornstarch on babies' butts (although some say it can promote a yeast-related rash), but the particles are larger and do not get into the lungs as talcum powders do.

- Avoid any powders.
    - They can cake on and then have to be wiped off, which is hard on irritated skin.

- Despite all of this if her parents insist, you may be using it!

Wipes

I had a stack of face cloths to clean my babies' butts, but baby wipes have come a long way. They are much milder and easier on babies' skin, and there are ones for sensitive skin. They come in more accessible packs that can be restocked and travel versions that can be reloaded for diaper bags.

> Some parents buy electric baby-wipe warmers. At first, I thought this excessive. I was very tempted to get one, in the winter, but did resist!

Some parents hem small squares of material (organic cotton, bamboo, or fleece) that are pre-soaked or wet as required. Most believe these are the most effective way to clean. I often get a facecloth rather than use a wipe if there is a poopy diaper for a newborn.

Potty Training

There are different methods of potty training: the one-day, the three-day, etc., so many that it is impossible to list them all.

Parents are now encouraged to "wait for signs of readiness" before toilet training. Some think this means waiting for their children to express the desire to use the toilet. However, for some children it can be as simple as recognizing that a wet diaper is uncomfortable.

Many put their child in regular underwear so she can feel the wetness and discomfort. This results in a few messy days and constant reinforcement of the methods used. The most important thing for you is to find out exactly what they are doing and how you can foster your grandchild's potty training.

> **Girl's usually potty train earlier than boys.**
>
> *My efforts to train my son rubbed off on my daughter. Despite the two-year difference in their ages, they trained at about the same time! I remember my daughter who didn't yet speak, dragging the potty for her big brother to use!*

There are potty chairs of many different kinds—musical potties, ones with every kind of cartoon character on them, special ones for boys' and girls'. They aren't expensive and can increase the chances of success all round.

They make liners for potty chairs so that you don't have to rinse out poopy potties. They also have plastic potties that fold up and to go in the diaper bag and disposable ones.

There are many different potty-training programs. My grandson will be experiencing the three-day method soon, so I cannot give a firsthand account yet. I will keep you posted.

> **A lot has changed in baby care.**
>
> *Watch, listen, and ask how you should do things while baby is in your care.*

8. BABY HEALTH AND SAFETY TODAY

A resounding fear among the women I talked with was health and safety of the grandbaby while in their care. Despite having raised my own and have cared for many young babies, this was a major worry of mine, too. This new grandchild is your child's most treasured joy, and you are responsible for her.... It's more daunting than one might think.

Safety starts in the hospital. Many hospitals have electronic transducers that are attached to the baby's umbilical cord or leg to ensure that the baby is not removed from the unit. Some hospitals will allow only one designated person to take the baby out of the room. They likely will not allow anyone to walk around with the baby; instead, they must use the bassinette, staff and parents have slipped and dropped babies. Some hospitals do not allow the baby to sleep in the mother's bed, as there have been baby deaths.

HEALTH

Normal wellness, growth and development, and special health situations are important for grandma to know more about.

Hearing

Our neighbors like to take their son to dirt-bike races; they had sound protective headphones for him from a very young age, but I have also seen other toddlers wearing earphones with music blaring or while playing games on various devices.

To protect your grandbaby's hearing:

- Do not expose the baby or growing child to undue noise (music, machinery).

    — Use ear protection, either earplugs or headphones (not earphones), if there will be a lot of noise.

Be alert for the following signs of hearing loss, even if the baby has been tested:

- Baby does not startle at loud noises.

- She does not turn to the source of a sound after six months of age.

- Baby does not say any single words by one year of age.

- She turns her head when she sees you but not when you call out her name.

> Not all children say "mama" or "dada" first, but saying any word by one year is an important milestone.

- Baby appears to hear some sounds, but not others.

Vision

You might have noticed more and younger children wearing glasses. A doctor will usually look inside the baby's eyes after birth. It is also recommended that babies get their eyes checked in the first year, usually around six months, and then at three and five years of age. This is especially important in babies who were born preterm. Signs of vision problems in children include the following:

> Early correction of eye problems in the first few years can lessen the chances of problems later on.

- Eye rubbing.

- Light sensitivity.

- Poor focusing or visual tracking (following an object).

- Abnormal alignment or movement of the eyes (after six months of age).

- Chronic eye redness or tearing.

- White pupils (cataracts) instead of black.

- Cross-eyed after the first three or four months.

Infection

As a caring grandmother, you will do all you can to help prevent infection. Babies do not show that they have an infection in the same way as adults. The changes can be subtle at first, but any baby with the following symptoms may have an infection and needs urgent help:

> Babies succumb to infection much more quickly than adults do, especially babies who are preterm, sick, or vulnerable in some way.

- Feeding or breathing problems.

- Slowing down—being lethargic or limp, especially if jaundiced.

- An unusual skin rash or a change in skin color (pale or mottled).

- Constant diarrhea.

- No urine or very dark urine.

- Crying, inability to settle, and unusual irritability.

One habit that my daughter assures is very annoying to her and her friends is people, including well-meaning grandparents, putting their unwashed finger into the baby's mouth to check for new teeth.

- Instead, if you want to see if there are any teeth, just look into the baby's mouth when she is crying.

- As my grandson got older, he was happy to open his mouth to show us his new teeth. This came in handy when he saw the dentist at two years of age.

> I cannot say it often enough: Wash your hands, especially before handling the baby.

Immunizations

Many of us were immunized as infants, and immunizations may be required for our jobs or for travel. Immunizations are another potential "hot spot" in families. Some parents do not immunize their children, and put their own babies and other babies, too young to get their shots, at risk for diseases.

A young couple I met surprised me when they refused to immunize their children. They were pleased to tell me their other children had not had any of the usual contagious diseases other children are immunized for (such as measles or meningitis). I explained to them that this was because most of the population has been immunized, which helps protect them (AKA "herd immunity"). The problem is that if enough people refuse immunization over time, it is just a matter of time before the disease rates increase. We are starting to see that happen with pertussis.

> Child immunization is a subject of debate in- and outside the medical community and within families.
>
> Research has disputed the notion that immunizations cause autism, yet the myth persists, and some parents refuse to immunize.

Pertussis: Pertussis (Whooping Cough) is a communicable (spreadable) disease, which has an unusual "whoop" cough. Whooping cough has resurfaced in North America and has led to the deaths of newborn babies.

My son was not immunized for pertussis because of a family

> One young woman said, *"You do want to minimize conflict with your grandfamily and respect their choices, but this is one area that it might be worth it for you to do additional research if the parents express a resistance toward immunization. It may be worth the life of your grandchild or another's child to press the issue."*

history of seizures (which was the guideline in 1979); he subsequently got whooping cough. I was pregnant with my daughter. All of my immunizations were up-to-date, and I did not get pertussis, which was good because I needed to care for my son, who "whooped" and coughed so hard that he vomited for weeks.

- Most mothers are offered the pertussis vaccine in the hospital now.
  - This is to help prevent spread to the baby, who is too young to be immunized.

- Others (i.e., fathers and grandparents) who provide care to the baby can also get a vaccination.

- Anyone with a latex allergy needs to get a special vaccine.

MILESTONES

It seems that everyone is obsessed with developmental milestones and will be asking how your grandchild is achieving them. The most frequently mentioned ones are "Is he sitting by himself?" "Can she crawl?" "Does she walk yet?" "Does he talk yet?"

If your grandchild is meeting all these achievements, then answering these questions is fine, and if your grandchild is ahead of the curve (the average baby), then you can burst with grandmotherly pride, but that is not always the case. Remember that many milestones have a wide range of ages in which to achieve them. It can be a source of embarrassment and worry for everyone in the family if a baby is not meeting particular milestone as expected.

Milestones are important indicators of developmental or neurological problems, and it is essential for parents to get the baby properly assessed and provided appropriate treatment if there is a significant delay. However, be sure to know what not meeting the milestones really means and understand why and when the parents (you, too) might start to worry about them.

If you kept your child's baby book up-to-date, this might be a very good time to take it out and see what your children were really achieving and at what age.

For example, babies usually stand around eight months and cruise around the furniture between nine and twelve months. Most are walking independently by fourteen or fifteen months old, but some healthy children do not walk until later. Experts do advise that babies who haven't walked independently by eighteen months need to be assessed.

Look to the parents' growth and development:

- When did your own child really walk, speak, get teeth, etc.?

- Give your child his or her own baby book.

  — It may just well be that your grandson is just like your son and is climbing the furniture at eight months or a late bloomer and isn't walking unassisted at seventeen months.

- Some baby sites provide email updates to inform parents of what they can expect and when to worry (See–Resources).

I used a developmental approach to raise my children. I had taken a child psychology course at university, but I referred most often to a white book, the name of which I cannot remember. I gave it as gifts for years. It spelled out development and behavior so clearly up to the first and second years that I always knew what to anticipate, how to encourage development, and what certain skills to watch for. It was very empowering to me as a new mother, and it meant that I rarely got frustrated with them about certain things that seemed to irritate other parents, such as drawing on the walls with crayons or insisting on dressing themselves! we know it's normal for children (or anyone) to act in certain ways at certain times in their lives, then we are all much better equipped to handle things when they do happen. baby development information is readily available through sites like www.babycenter.com or www.babycentre.ca.

Babies are usually assessed for developmental achievements during regular medical checkups or immunizations. This can be done so informally that the parents don't even realize that it's happening. Sometimes parents are given questionnaires to complete that compare the child to others their age.

> One new grandmother was exasperated, *"My daughter cannot tolerate to hear Sadie (ten-months-old) cry. She holds her all the time, during naps (because the baby may wake up) and until she is fully asleep at night. She wears the baby in a carrier to do her chores and everywhere she goes. She is exhausted and has a very limited social life because the baby won't go to sleep for anyone else or anywhere else. I know she feels trapped, but she won't let us help."*

Shaken Baby Syndrome

Shaken baby syndrome (SBS) is a triad of symptoms that include bleeding of the brain (subdural hematoma), blood in the eyes (retinal hemorrhage), and swelling of the brain (cerebral edema). SBS is thought to be caused by excessive shaking of a young child by an adult.

- SBS is seen more in children of young, inexperienced, and socially stressed parents, but anyone who is caring for a fussy baby can shake a baby too hard.

- If they feel they are going to lose their temper with the baby, we advise parents and care providers to place the baby in a crib or play yard and leave the room or go outside and call someone to come and care for the baby.

> If you get a distraught call to attend to your grandchild, recognize that your child may be at his or her wits' end and is reaching out for help. *Don't judge. Go if you can or ask someone else to help.*

SLEEP AND SLEEP SAFETY

Sleep is one of the areas of great change that you need to learn about because chances are you will care for your grandchild, so you need to understand why and how to maintain safe sleep.

Sudden Infant Death Syndrome

Sudden infant death syndrome (SIDS) is the number one cause of death in healthy babies under a year old; even so, it is rare with the peak age between two and four months of age. We don't fully understand the cause of SIDS, but it is believed to be associated with a baby's inability to wake up (sleep arousal), failure to sense a build-up of carbon dioxide in her blood, and lack of ability to regulate body temperature leading to overheating.

- There are other factors associated with SIDS, such as smoking around the baby, not breastfeeding, being a teenage mother, and the child being exposed to infection.

- The number of babies dying from SIDS has decreased drastically since parents have put their babies on their backs to sleep.

I know of one family who tragi-cally lost their grandson to SIDS. This

> Cribs need to be firm, bumper pads are not advised, and no heavy blankets or quilts are used in the crib.

was the third baby born to a healthy, educated family who did everything properly and had no risk factors. The father put the four-month-old baby down for his afternoon nap in the crib in their bedroom upstairs. The baby monitor was on, and he was downstairs playing with the older children. After the baby had been quietly sleeping for a long time, he went to wake him up. He had died. As you can imagine, the entire family was devastated. They had taken all the precautions any family would, and still the worst happened.

"Back to Sleep"

You likely put your babies to sleep on their sides supported by rolled blankets at first, and then on their stomachs with their head turned to one side, as they got older. In those days, we never wanted ba-bies on their back, as we believed baby would choke if she spit up. Everything changed in the mid-

> Since the back-to-sleep initiatives started, the rate of SIDS has decreased by fifty percent!

1990s and now all parents are told to have baby sleep on her back.

There have been many "back-to-sleep" campaigns by government and health groups worldwide. The goal is to help prevent SIDS—and it's working.

- A baby with balding is still perceived by some as being left unattended for prolonged periods, but it can happen quickly if the baby sleeps on a firm surface (as advised).

Flathead

An effect of babies sleeping on their backs is the possible development of flat spots on the back or on the side of the head. Almost fifty percent of babies now have 'flatspots.'

- Brachycephaly or "flathead" and plagiocephaly (flatness on one side of the head) can happen in any baby and is becoming increasingly common.

When my grandson was about six weeks old, my daughter noticed a flat spot developing on his head and noticed that he held his head to one side more, even when we tried to move it. We were shocked that this happened because he was rarely left on his back other than to sleep. He was never left in his car seat even when sleeping peacefully, and the length of any walks was curtailed to avoid him lying in the stroller.

We were vigilant, doing everything we could to keep the pressure off his head and to ease the tightness in his neck muscles that was causing it to pull to one side. He attended a head clinic and did physical therapy for months. With a lot of work and resourcefulness by my daughter and her husband, his head improved greatly.

Despite this, some uneducated people made hurtful and mean comments about the shape of his head! Now a smart little guy with a very full head of hair, the shape of his head is neither noticeable nor important anymore, but we did worry.

Here is what you need to know about "flathead":

- No one knows why some babies get flathead or and why boys are more susceptible.

- Limit the length of time that baby lies on her back or in a car seat or stroller because that position is thought to contribute to the shape of the baby's head.

- Each night the parents can switch the end of the crib the baby's head is at, as she will naturally turn its head to see her mother.

- Most babies will outgrow plagiocephaly once they are more mobile and roll over in their sleep, but it can take up to two years to change the shape of the head.

- There are often special head clinics to assess and correct the problem.

- In some babies, the deformity is so great that helmets or banding devices are used to reshape the skull. This is difficult for the parents-they will need your support.

- Physical therapists can suggest exercises to promote evenness in the skull and movement of the neck.

- Special positioning pillows designed to keep the head in a certain position can also cause suffocation, so only use as prescribed by a pediatrician.

When we were in China before back sleeping campaigns had started here. I noticed that everyone had a flat head. The couple we traveled with was Chinese and had a son who was born in Canada in the late 1980s, so he had a very round head from sleeping on his stomach, as was advised here at the time. The mother told me that when she first took him home as a toddler, their relatives were horrified that he had a round head, not flat (much as North Americans are often disturbed by the sight of a flathead). Babies in China, Japan, and some African countries have always slept on their backs, and the beds are much, much firmer than ours are—they expect that babies will have flat heads.

> *Many believe that we, in North America, will adapt to the look of a more flat or irregular shaped head in a generation or two.*

Baby and Apnea Monitors

Baby monitors have come a long way. Some have multiple receivers and little cameras that allow you to see or hear the baby make noise wherever you are in the house. However wonderful the technology has become, I fear that these monitors give us a false of security. The baby I mentioned earlier who died of SIDS had a functioning baby monitor. It might have alerted a parent to a choking or crying baby, but sadly, it did not let the father know that his baby wasn't sleeping soundly as he thought, but had quietly died.

Some parents also purchase apnea monitors. Apnea is a cessation of breathing. Apnea monitors have electrode pads that are attached to the baby. They are designed to alert the parents if the baby stops breathing or if her heart stops beating. Preterm babies are often put on apnea monitors in the hospital and may come home with them. Some babies may have blue spells or even apnea spells, and the parents are advised to monitor them during sleep or whenever they are unattended.

It is unlikely that a normal, term baby would require an apnea monitor, but if a family has lost a baby to SIDS, it might help them feel more secure. Parents can buy a mattress pad that has an alarm that will sound if the baby doesn't breathe or move for twenty seconds. Unfortunately, babies can set these monitors off often when there is no cause for concern and can disrupt the parent's precious sleep.

If parents want a monitor, they will need to ensure it's of good quality.

- Resist the urge to buy, unless the parents pick out the brand/ type.

Co-Sleeping and Bedsharing

There are many different interpretations and definitions of "co-sleeping" and "bedsharing." For some, co-sleeping means sleeping in the same bed or on the same surface with the baby, but for the AAP, it means being in the same room. This gets confusing because, while pediatric experts support co-sleeping, most do not endorse "bedsharing" (the baby sleeping in the same bed as adults).

We know that parents in many cultures bedshare, and it is increasing in popularity in North America, but there is a higher incidence of SIDS in babies who bedshare, particularly if the parents drink alcohol or bedshare for longer times at night (e.g., eight hours compared to twenty minutes for a feed and cuddle). Babies are more likely to be injured or die, from falling out of bed or by being trapped between the mattress and the wall, if they sleep with their parent(s) all night.

If your children are bedsharing, here are the facts:

- Many attachment-parenting advocates strongly promote bedsharing until the child wants her own bed; however, most pediatric professionals do not support bedsharing.

> **Bedsharing threatened one mother-daughter relationship:** *"They were practising attachment parenting. Breastfeeding was not going well; Jen was exhausted and depressed. She wanted to have the baby close by for night feeds, so had her in bed with them. I said I was worried about one of them rolling on her or, at worst, accidentally killing her. Jen was furious. But, one night after her husband found himself rolling onto the baby, she was quickly put to sleep in her own bassinette."* **Baby was then co-sleeping, but no longer bedsharing.**

- Bedsharing arrangements are most dangerous to the baby if the parents have consumed alcohol or other substances or smoke.

- Younger babies are more at risk to die from SIDS while bedsharing.

- Advocates of bedsharing claim that babies fall back to sleep more quickly and keep warmer.

- It is advised for babies to co-sleep—that is to sleep in the parents' room—for the first six months. This usually means having all of the baby change equipment, rocking chair, etc., close by!

  — Parents should have the bassinette or crib in the room next to or close to, their bed or they can use special co-sleeping cribs that attach to the side of the bed and prevent the parent from rolling onto the baby because the crib is only a little larger than the baby is.

- If they bedshare, the baby is not to be under the covers with them.

  — There should be no pillows close to the baby.

  — The mattress should be firm.

While my friend's grandson slept in a beautiful bassinette beside his parents for those important first six months, her granddaughter, born two years later, was a particularly noisy sleeper. She grunted and made noises all night long. The bassinette was soon moved into the walk-in closet! She was still close enough that they could attend to her quickly, but they didn't have to hear every single sound the baby made, which let them have much deserved sleep.

> As cozy as it sounds and essential as it is to the health of the baby to have her close by, it can also be very disruptive to both parents' sleep if the baby is a noisy sleeper.
>
> *New mothers now may be more tired than we were with our babies in their own decorated nursery down the hall.*

Sleep Sacs

A couple whose first child died from SIDS created "sleep sacs" to avoid the use of a blanket that could possibly lead to suffocation and yet keep baby warm. Some sleep sacs swaddle the baby while others have straps at the shoulder and just a sack at the bottom for full movement of the legs. There are concerns that babies can overheat, but the AAP currently promotes sleep sacs as a way of keeping babies warm without covering their heads. There are different thicknesses of sleep sacs for different weather conditions. My friend's grandchildren, ages three and four, still sleep in their sleep sacs. If they are ever in a sack race, they will surely win!

Sleep Training

We likely put our babies down for a nap, closed the door, and went to do chores. Our mothers probably put us outside in a pram for an hour, rain or shine. Now there are hypersensitive baby monitors to amplify every sound in the baby's room, and many believe that parents (and grandparents) have become hypervigilant.

If the baby continues to cry and wants to eat, parents may try to find a way to have her sleep throughout the night.

- Sleep training involves a series of techniques designed to get the baby to sleep through the night.

- The approach the parents have decided to use, such as the Weissbluth method, which promotes using bed and naptime rituals, will determine what you will do to help your grandchild go to sleep.

- Support the parents in whatever they are trying to do.

  > A young baby will eat every few hours around the clock, but by six months of age or twelve-pound weight, she will sleep for longer periods without eating throughout the night.
  >
  > Parents can then "sleep train."

  — One of the most important things with any type of sleep training method is consistency.

  — Recognize that, even if they are choosing to follow a method that allows crying, they can feel guilty about letting the baby cry for any period. Be supportive of their choices – they may be choosing them out of desperation and not desire.

  — Or, if they choose not to sleep train and the baby is still waking often, they may be exhausted and need your help.

- I found some videos on YouTube by Dana Oberman that seem sensible to me http://www.youtube.com/watch?v=CWvvlu3-VE4&feature=related. If your grandchild's parents ask for help, you could mention them.

Some parents hire professional sleep services that guarantee that the baby will sleep within a certain amount of time. Often there is in-

> It is clear that no matter what method is used, everyone needs to stick to it for some time for it to work.

home, overnight, support and follow-up. They are costly. I haven't heard any firsthand experiences, but for parents who need their sleep and have tried absolutely everything, it might be a worthwhile investment. Other parents try white noise or special baby sleep machines that mimic the sounds of the womb or other gentle sounds, they can be within sheep and other stuffed animals.

Crying It Out

The "crying it out" (CIO) approach assumes that being able to fall asleep on the baby's own is a skill like any other skill and that the baby can master this if given the opportunity. People often think that this method of sleep training involves leaving babies alone to cry for as long as it takes before they fall asleep. But CIO seems to describe any sleep training approach—and there are many—that say that it's OK to let a baby cry for a specified time (often a very short period of time) before offering her comfort.

Some parents or grandparents are not comfortable with CIO, especially if they follow the attachment-parenting philosophy (See–Attachment Parenting). These parents may follow the advice set out by Elizabeth Pantley in *The No Cry Sleep Solution,* which is recommended by Dr. Sears and La Leche League.

> *"Sleep-training" is another topic of potential dispute between parents and grandparents.*
>
> *You may have blocked out the number of sleepless nights spent trying to get your own children to sleep through the night!*

In his 1985 book *Solve Your Child's Sleep Problems* (revised in 2006), pediatrician Richard Ferber presented one method of getting children to sleep that has become virtually synonymous with CIO—so much so that you'll hear parents refer to any CIO method as "Ferberizing." A bath, teeth brushing, and having a book read are all part of the Ferber method.

Sound familiar? That's probably because it's how we likely got our children to sleep! Whatever method the parents have chosen, agree, or not, babies like routine. Once they can talk, children will often ask for specifics of their routine (what book to read and where to read it, when to brush teeth, anything that they do), and then try follow the routine as carefully as possible. Recent research has reported that routines are good for baby's brain development.

When I babysit, I am very keen that my daughter does not come home to a crying child. Routines do change as the baby grows, so I am careful to ask each time what to do when my grandson is going to bed for a nap or for the night. I realized one night as my older grandson was in his crib and I was leaving the room that I had read his favorite books, but I didn't know what his parents said as they left the room. I would

> **Always ask about sleep routines and follow them carefully.**
>
> *Routines and rituals are very important.*

always say "night-night" to my children. I smiled to learn from my daughter that his sleep routine also involved "night-night."

Cribs and Sleep Surfaces

Cribs have changed. The railings do not come down, and the height of the mattress is adjustable usually to two heights: high for the infant stage and low for when they are pulling themselves up (with the goal of avoiding them climbing over and running amok at five in the morning).

Not all babies have cribs these days; some parents continue to bedshare until the child is ready for a bed, and some sleep in a family bed for many years.

The low setting on many cribs is now much lower than before. They are great for keeping little climbers in their crib for a few months longer, but I am short, and this low level is a huge issue when I try to put my grandson into his crib to sleep or to pick him up if he is fussing.

The latest rules for crib safety include the following:

- No bumper pads.

  — They are a smothering risk and I am not sure why they are allowed to sell them. Resist the urge to buy.

  — An informed daughter or daughter-in-law will throw them away; you might have been offended had you not been reading this!

  — "Breathable" bumper pads are available; however, there have been injuries from babies being tangled in the ties or launching themselves out of the crib from the pads.

- No toys in the crib.

  — Filling the crib with all of the child's stuffed animals and other toys is a smothering hazard, or children can step on them to propel themselves over the crib sides.

The rate of SIDS has decreased, but at the same time, the rate of death from other things related to sleep has increased.

It is recommended that babies have nothing in the crib, but a loosely wove blanket will help to prevent smothering.

- Do not use plastic mattress pads or covers; special breathable mattresses and covers are available to help prevent SIDS.

Tummy Time

Because babies are put to sleep on their backs, they also need to have short periods of <u>supervised</u> "tummy time" every day. Tummy time involves putting the baby on her stomach to strengthen her neck and upper body. Tummy time is essential for the development of crawling skills. Supervised babies can also lie on their sides, supported by a roll or towels to avoid unnecessary pressure on the neck or head.

Tummy time is important and something that you may be asked to do with the baby. Keep the following in mind:

- Start for very short periods of time (a minute).

- Some babies like tummy time; others get very upset and take longer to get used to it.

- The length of tummy time increases gradually over time.

- Do not put the baby on her tummy right after she has eaten.

- The young baby can be on your lap or on a quilt on the floor.

- Put toys close by to stimulate the baby to move.

- You can lie on the floor with the baby on your tummy and sing songs or talk to her.

- You can try to put a pad under the baby's chest and support her chin to help strengthen her neck. Everything is done gradually and gently.

> The baby must be in full view of adult during tummy time or when lying on her side.

- Once the baby is lifting her head unsupported, you can help strengthen her upper body by putting the baby's arms and hands in a sitting-up position to encourage her to lift her upper body.

- You can turn the older baby over and help her learn to roll over.

Home Safety

As much as grandmothers worried about safety, your house can pose real danger to baby. Your house is full of your prized possessions and everyday items, but if you want to have your grandchildren over, it makes sense that you must do some childproofing your house.

Remember that little babies aren't coordinated. Don't prop them up on couches or counters when you are doing things, no matter how easy or safe it might seem or how old they are. It might look cute in photos, but they can topple over very quickly.

I was making toast for my grandson one day. He wasn't happy when I went to put him down. My shoulder was uncomfortable, so I put him on the counter, holding him with my hand. When I was reaching for the toaster, he leaned forward and he burned his finger. Fortunately, it was a small burn, but it was his first injury. I learned the hard way always to be vigilant.

Safety Latches

We may have used elastic bands to keep cupboards closed (like I did when my first grandson started getting around), but it is best to be safe rather than sorry when it comes to dangerous products that may be lurking in your cupboards or even garbage that you hadn't considered might contain noxious products.

Plug protectors and cupboard and drawer stop devices have changed. They are much more complex now, and you may have some difficulty figuring out how to apply them or circumvent them if you need to open a door! There are various kinds of gadgets for this. When I went shopping for ours, I could tell there were some that would give me grief to open.

One friend's grandchildren are on their third variety of door latch. Their latest one is magnetic, and requires the adult to get a magnetic key hanging on the fridge to release the cupboards. She says it's a challenge to open for her, but the children aren't able to do so yet, so that is good.

> Be sure you know how to open (and close) all of the doors in your grandfamily's home and your own home, too!

We had a lesson about safety when my grandson locked himself in the bathroom at nineteen months of age. Of course, once he realized that he was unable to get out, he was very upset. My daughter could not open the door, even with a screwdriver. I was away. My son-in-law had to come home from work and drill the door off its hinges to get him out. We found out later that new homes or homes with new doors have a special screwdriver to open locked doors now, ask your child where his is. Apparently, a thin crochet hook will work well, too, but not many women crochet anymore!

Water Temperature

You may like washing your dishes and laundry in very hot water and can easily add cold water as needed for your personal use. However, a young child can just turn on a tap and may not be able to get out of the tub or sink in which hot water is running, which can result in a bad burn if the water is too hot. To be safe, check the temperature setting on your water heater. Set your water heater's thermostat to 120° F (48° C) or lower.

Pets

Your children moved out and your nest is empty, so your husband brings you home a little fluffy bundle of white cuteness for your birthday, maybe a fluffy white Shih-Tzu puppy. You love the dog and spoil it rotten. Suddenly, there is competition in the form of a cute little baby.

> **Pets can be jealous as you show attention to grand-children.**
>
> *Be very careful not to leave children and pets together alone.*

The dog I had when my children were born was a very patient, lovely mutt, but her personality changed once my son started crawling. One day my son backed her into a corner as he cruised along. She jumped over him and was edgy from that day on (despite his efforts to feed her from his high chair). We had only cats when my grandson came along. As soon as he was mobile, I moved their food and water and had to remember to close the door to their litter box! A cat door works well.

Your grandchild getting into dog or cat food is a minor consequence of having pets compared to the potential for injuries. Dogs can bite; cats can scratch. The Centers for Disease Control and Prevention (CDC) tells us what might be obvious—that, as the number of dogs in the home increases, so does the chance of being bit. Adults with two or more dogs in the household are five times more likely to be bitten than those living without any dogs in the home. If you have more than one pet, you need to be even more vigilant when your grandchildren are around.

Poisons

Because we are older, we are more likely to be taking various pills that could be dangerous to a young child. Medications are not the only items that need to be keep off limits:

- Vitamins, especially those with iron, can be toxic to a toddler.

- Keep medications out of reach, not on the dining room table in a basket!

- Put detergent pods (those new laundry and dishwasher pods of liquid or powdered detergent) and other kitchen supplies out of reach.

> One day, I heard my daughter telling my grandson, "Go show Gammie." He toddled down the hall to show me a detergent pod in his hand! We had put on the door latches, but I had been emptying the recycling bin and hadn't closed the door.
>
> **They are up high now.**

Other Safety Risks

When the strangulation risk of window blinds and cords to children hit the news years ago, you may not have had young children or grandchildren and may not have worried about it, but children still die this way every year. If you are putting a crib in a room not intended for a baby, be sure the window coverings are safe. Better yet, if possible, avoid putting the baby close to a window at all. Batteries, particularly those small button batteries, sometimes found in musical cards or children's' toys, have led to serious injuries and death in children.

- You may not even realize a child has swallowed a battery at first because she may just have a tummy ache, but the substances inside batteries can burn a hole inside a child's esophagus and stomach.

Check the magnets on your fridge or message board. Are they small and powerful? While you may find them very useful, a child who swallows more than one of them could end up having very painful intestinal surgery as it has happened that magnets in different parts of a child's digestive system can stick together.

> **One young mother exclaimed,** "I asked her [MiL] repeatedly to not put her mug of hot coffee on the floor. Aiden was crawling all over. We just got to him, as he was ready to pull it onto himself. It was very frightening to him and us. I wish she would just listen to me."

- Move magnets entirely out of reach or exchange with larger safer magnets.

There are many checklists available that you might want to use when you baby-proof your home, such as http://www.hc-sc.gc.ca/cps-spc/pubs/cons/child-enfant/safe-securite-eng.php.

The Centers for Disease Control have a variety of excellent fact sheets that address many different areas of recreational and home safety at http://www.cdc.gov/safechild.

Exposure to Smoke

Second- and thirdhand smoking—any kind of smoke—is a no-no around babies, particularly in enclosed areas such as homes and cars.

> *Having a new grandbaby might be a good incentive for everyone around her to quit smoking.*

Babies breathe faster than adults do, consequently they inhale more; therefore, it is important to limit their exposure to smoke.

Appreciate that:

- Secondhand smoke is a combination of smoke from the burning end of a cigarette, pipe, or cigar and the smoke exhaled from the lungs of the person who smoked it into the environment.

  — It is associated with SIDS, lung infections, and asthma.

  — Children are trapped where the adults are smoking; they can't leave the environment.

- Thirdhand smoke is smoke that is trapped in the fabric, furniture, walls, and objects around them in rooms and cars where people usually smoke, even if they are not smoking anymore.

  — Thirdhand smoke also gets into household dust, which babies swallow when they put their hands in their mouths.

  — Because they breathe more quickly and also crawl on the floor or furniture and put their hands in their mouths, babies can inhale or ingest twenty times more thirdhand smoke chemicals (like lead and arsenic) than adults do.

- If you do smoke, do it outside and away from the baby (not in confined areas like homes and cars), and wash your hands after you smoke and before you handle the baby.

- If you smoke inside your house, you may find your child will not want to bring your grandbaby over. Don't be offended–recognize that they are doing it for the health of the baby.

Sun Safety

Babies can become sunburned within fifteen minutes of being out in the sun and can quickly become dehydrated from overheating. Overexposure to the sun as a child is linked to skin cancer and cataracts later in life.

Precautions are needed to avoid too much sun:

- Sunscreen needs to be high SPF 60 (sun protection factor).

- Better sunscreens contain zinc and are free of parabens, PABA, and titanium dioxide.

149

- Apply sunscreen before putting on insect repellent. Do not use combination sunscreen/insect repellents, as sunscreen needs to be reapplied more often than insect repellents.

> **Baby sunglasses can be strapped onto baby's head.**
>
> *This is very important if the baby is in a car seat or stroller and can't move away from the sunlight.*

- Sunscreen isn't used on babies under six months of age; rather, keep them out of direct sun altogether. Some doctors advise waiting until the baby is twelve months old.

> **Choose wide-brimmed hats. Fortunately, most babies look adorable in hats.**
>
> *If baby resists wearing a hat, wear one yourself to making it more desirable to the baby.*

- Avoid putting baby in the direct sun, particularly between 11 a.m. and 4 p.m.

- Keep the baby covered with a hat, an umbrella, or a stroller cover for protection.

- The baby also can get protection from light-colored clothing or a non-toxic sun-protection suit for swim and play.

Insect Repellent

As I write this chapter, the first reports of the year are in for West Nile Virus in our area. West Nile Virus is carried by the small *Culex quinquefasciatus* mosquito. West Nile causes flu-like symptoms and can result in encephalitis (inflammation of the brain, with symptoms such as fever, headache, vomiting, and confusion).

> **Citronella is associated with lung problems and deaths.**
>
> *Never use citronella oils or candles close to a baby less than six-months-old.*

It appears that babies and pregnant women are at no greater risk from mosquito-borne infections than other people are, but protection is needed to prevent exposure to those and other insects:

- Read the label, most repellents are not recommended for babies under six months, and have limited (once/day) use for toddlers.

- Try to use non-chemical protection where possible:
    — Screens on windows and netting on strollers.
    — "Bug" shirts provide good coverage for everyone.

Is Baby Choking or Gagging?

With the trend toward babies feeding themselves adult food and less of the pureed baby foods, choking and gagging are a concern. On the plus side, because most parents do wait till six months to introduce solids and because they often skip the spoon-feeding stage, most babies will not have their gag reflexes overridden and may be able to handle pieces of food better than you would have expected your own children to have done so.

> **Gagging is** *a protective reflex that helps prevent food or other objects from going down the esophagus.*
>
> **Choking** *means the airway is completely obstructed.*

One of my nurse friends with a young granddaughter worried about knowing the difference between choking and gagging. This is a healthy fear to have. It is important to know that choking and gagging are two different things.

- Gagging is the result of stimulating the gag reflex, a protective reflex that helps prevent food or other objects from going down our esophagus.
    — Babies often gag, cough, or sputter while they are learning to eat solids, sometimes with their eyes watering or a surprised expression on their face.

- Choking is a serious situation for anyone. It happens when the airway is completely obstructed, and the obstruction prevents air from reaching the lungs.
    — A choking baby cannot cry or talk, will quickly become pale and blue, and may lose consciousness and become limp.

The most important thing is to try to avoid choking in the first place. Keep them seated at a table while eating rather than while running around. Encourage them to eat slowly and chew their food well if they can understand.

Infants put whatever they are given in their mouths, so you need to be careful that you cut up foods that are firm and round and can cause obstruction of the airway and choking.

- Don't give babies too much food at one time, even if it is in small chunks – a handful of shredded cheese can obstruct the airway.

> **The major cause of choking in young children is food.**
>
> *Watch young children while they eat.*

- Hot dogs and sausages are a choking hazard for babies.

  — If, with the parent's permission, you decide to feed your grandchild hot dogs or sausage, remove the skin and cut lengthwise and then into small pieces.

- Cut whole grapes, large blueberries, pitted cherries, and cherry tomatoes into quarters or smaller.

- Cut vegetables into small strips or pieces that are not round.

- Squish peas, not just because it lessens the choking hazard, but also because it is the best way for the baby to get nutrients from them.

- Cut toast, crackers, and cheese into small cubes.

- Avoid hard or sticky candy and popcorn.

- Avoid nuts and seeds because the baby can inhale them.

- Ice cubes are a significant choking hazard.

The Choking Baby

If you think a baby is choking on something, it is important not to stick your fingers in her mouth because it may cause the object to go down and further obstruct the airway. Instead:

1. Sit down, if possible.

2. Use gravity.

3. Hold the baby's face down and with her head lower than her body, draped over your forearm. It is best to rest even small babies on your arm on your thigh.

4. Thump the infant gently but firmly about five times on the upper middle of the back using the heel of your hand.

   — These back blows should release the food causing the choking.

5. If nothing comes out or if you do not see anything.

   — Do not poke your fingers around in the mouth.

6. Flip the baby over onto the forearm of your other arm.

   — Keep the baby's head lower than her body.

7. Open the baby's mouth.

   — If you can see something, use your little finger to hook it out.

   — If it is very slippery or feels like it might go down, stop immediately.

8. Use two fingers placed at the center of the infant's breastbone, between the nipples.

   — Give her five quick chest compressions with two fingers.

9. Keep doing back blows and flipping the baby over for chest thrusts until you see something in her mouth or she coughs something up.

   — If the baby is coughing up, turn her head over and down.

   — Usually, this is enough to bring up the choking item.

10. If the object comes out and the baby does not start to breathe right away, have someone call 911, or you call them.

    — Check the inside of the upper arm for a heartbeat

— If there is no heart rate, start CPR.

— If the baby has an adequate heartbeat (~100 bpm), but isn't breathing, do rescue breathing, which is putting your mouth over the baby's mouth and nose and breathing in about forty times a minute.

CPR—Cardio Pulmonary Resuscitation

I have been a CPR instructor for almost thirty years and used the skills a few times in my personal life. One day while shopping with my toddler son, he started coughing and choking on a cookie. It was a horrifying situation because he stopped breathing and went very tense, then started turning cyanotic (blue).

> Being able to perform CPR is a skill that won't just necessarily help with your grandchildren, as your family and friends' age their chances of having a stroke or heart attack increase.

I struggled to get him out of the shopping cart to turn him upside down to try to remove the cookie. I was pregnant at the time, and it wasn't easy because he was panicking. I finally got him out, turned him over, and pounded his back. His color returned after he expelled a large amount of phlegm and cookie. Store employees and shoppers just stood staring. Although I should have asked for help, I was just panicked to help him. An awful experience could have had a terrible outcome if I had not known what to do.

> Calling 911 is essential if some-
> one is unconscious, but what if
> you are camping or the weath-
> er is bad? You need to know
> how to help.

Should the worst happen and your grandchild loses consciousness or stops breathing, what will you do? The better prepared you are, the less you will panic.

Learning infant or adult CPR, which includes how to use an Automated External Defibrillator (AED) and to care for someone who is choking, are skills that you might consider mastering. This is particularly true if you are a cottager or for any reason have no immediate source of emergency services available to help you.

- The American Heart Association offers courses designed for people who want to be able to know what to do: Family & Friends CPR Anytime® is a course that includes infant, child, and adult CPR, use of the defibrillator, and choking.

  — You can take the infant part of the course separately, which will take about a half an hour, but including the child and adult sections takes only an hour longer and will prepare you to help save the life of someone close to you.

- In Canada, you can take the Heartsaver AED course, which also includes CPR, the AED, and choking in infants, children, and adults, including pregnant women.

  — The courses are often available through your local Heart and Stroke Association, community groups, or colleges.

  — They don't appear to offer these courses just for the infant.

There are videos of infant and adult CPR online, but from what I can see, they appear to offer only a short clip of the skills. They don't tell you how to know what to do and when to do it. Use the online clips only after you have completed the course or if there are no courses in your area.

> If possible, take a proper CPR or safety course with a certified instructor where you can practice the skills and become confident in how to do CPR.

9. Equipment Now

Something for Everyone

One walk through a baby store or the baby section of a department store and you will be amazed at the overwhelming number of devices and baby equipment that are out there. The colors are amazing, too, from traditional baby-soft hues to bold, bright colors. But, color is only one consideration; the most important thing has to be safety.

- Two major sources to check are:

- The Consumer Product Safety Commission: http://www.cpsc.gov/.

- Health Canada: http://www.hc-sc.gc.ca/cps-spc/pubs/cons/child-enfant/index-eng.php.

Car Seats

Car accidents are the number one cause of death in children one to twelve years old. Car seats were mostly optional for our children, but now law requires them because they are the best way to protect children.

Many hospitals do not allow the parents to take their baby home in a vehicle without knowing how to fit baby properly in the seat.

- Babies are put in a rear-facing car seat in the back seat as recommended by the National Highway Traffic Safety Administration.

- Air bags going off can harm the baby.

- Parents often post a mirror at the back so that they can see the baby.

> *Stay alert to baby in the car: Three babies recently died after being left in car seats in hot weather—two of them in the care of their grandmother, who was in her fifties. Thirty-two babies died left in cars in the US in 2012.*
>
> **Put your purse in the back seat with baby.**

You need to make sure the baby is in correctly and that it is secured properly.

- If there are two of you, it is best to double-check that the other person has secured the baby in the car seat.

- Always remember to check the car when leaving it to make sure there isn't a baby in there.

- Miscommunications or changes in routine have led to babies being left in the car, resulting in tragedy.

You can't just pick up a used car seat. It needs to be assessed because the weight and height of the baby determines what kind of seat is needed. On a recent walk through the baby section of a national department store, I counted more than thirty different kinds of infant car seats. This is in addition to ones that are part of "travel systems." Also, car seats expire because of the

> *Car seats have come a long way, and the safety features and requirements continue to evolve all the time.*

> I am mortified to tell you that while my daughter and I were busy running errands one day, we somehow left my grandson in his car seat unstrapped. She usually liked to make sure it was tight enough when I would put him in, so I didn't buckle him up, leaving it up to her to strap him, and I got into the passenger seat. She assumed I had buckled him in. When we got home, a short distance away, we found that he had quietly slid down and was standing on the floor as surprised as we were.

breakdown of plastic materials used in the construction. Be sure the car seat you are using is still current.

Travel systems are strollers with the car seat attached. The car seat can be removed and carried into the house or put in the car. The stroller can be upright or reclined, but there can be limitations to the overall function when a product tries to do everything.

Strollers

Strollers can be a very expensive and confusing purchase. There are a multitude of types and models. I wanted to have a stroller at my house. I found my grandson's stroller, which was part of a travel system, to be awkward to put in and take out of my daughter's car or turn around corners.

I noticed many people in our area using "chariot"-style strollers while they ran and walked. I looked up the different brands online and visited my local bicycle store. The owner told me that if I bought one, I would have no trouble selling it, and some used ones sold for the same price as a new one. I went home, checked online, and saw one mildly used stroller for less than half the price of one in the store. This was the first second-hand purchase I have made online, and I was pleased with the outcome! Since then I have bought a similar double stroller, using the same online process. When I arrived to get the stroller, it was a grandmother selling it, having used it for her grandchildren too!

When it comes to strollers, note:

- "High-end" does seem to make a difference. With one trip around the store, you will understand the benefits of having wheels that swivel around and not just point forward.

- The fancier strollers have special wheels for those who like to run or for attaching the stroller to a bicycle or skis and slings for infants.

Walkers/Highchairs/Seats

Walkers: While your little ones may have cruised throughout the house in their walker, but your grandchild is not likely to. Walkers are a leading cause of injury in infants, with stairs mostly to blame, even with adults close by. They are believed to hinder, rather than promote walking because they favor strengthening of the lower half of the body, while the upper half is not developing at the same rate.

Given the safety concerns, is it any wonder that pediatricians discourage the use of walkers and that their sale has been banned in Canada since 2004? Nowadays, babies can enjoy "stationary baby centers" or "saucers."

- They can sit and play with a variety of toys and often spin around or bounce a bit, but the unit is not mobile, so there is no risk of cruising down the stairs.

- If you feel that your grandchild must have a walker, avoid buying ones at garage sales. There are newer walkers on the market intended to be wide enough so that they do not fit through doors, thereby containing the baby to one room.

  — They also have a device to help prevent falls down the stairs.

Highchairs: If baby eats at your house and if she is exploring her food, you will want a highchair with a removable tray (removes from the table part) to wash off the food! There are also good plastic highchairs that attach to a chair that parents can take when they eat out. I bought an antique high chair, with no tray that snugs right up to the table. We use a placemat. We had to improvise with towels when he was little, but I like it because it fits with our décor. Also our cats feel quite proper sitting in it when my grandson isn't here!

Seats: popular to contain the younger baby who cannot sit alone is the "Bumbo" or other similar device with molded plastic or rubber seats. These seats have a high back and legs that keep the baby in. Bumbos come with a little tray and are handy for taking with you while you are visiting if there is no high chair. My grandson liked his and it was very helpful to give him time sitting upright and not putting pressure on his head.

The Bumbo recalled last year out of concern for babies fracturing their skulls.

- Parents who already own a Bumbo need to get a special kit from the manufacturer.

- As with car seats, do not leave babies either unattended or on a high surface where they can fall off.

- Chubby babies may have difficulty with the leg holes as they age.

- While they show toddlers using them on the package, there is now a toddler booster Bumbo seat.

Playpens/Play Yards

When I had my first child, I was given a playpen. I didn't use it often. I left the side down, and it was used mostly to store toys at night. With my second child, I occasionally put the side up when I had to do something outside or wanted to keep my children out of things, and they didn't seem to mind or even notice sometimes. As they got older, they would voluntarily go in there to play with toys.

Now, some consider playpens to be like a prison, with children "penned" in; hence, the name has changed from playpens to "play yards", I suppose. The major function of the play yard/pen is the same: to keep the baby in one spot. But, as with all things, there have been many changes!

- They are smaller, but taller.

- The sides are unlikely to come down unless for packing up

A friend got a play yard exactly like the one at her grandbaby's house—so, naps at grandma's house are uneventful!

- Some have a handy change table, bassinette/nap area with music and movement features to keep a young baby happy and able to stay in the living area during the day.

- If the baby will sleep in it, they can sleep rested when they travel, including to your house!

- Hotels may say they provide a crib, but often it's a play yard, so parents need to ensure that they get what they really want when booking a room.

Gates

The apprehension about baby gates hasn't changed since our day. No matter how well gates are designed, some babies are challenged to figure out how to climb over and drop to the other side! Today's parents may or may not use gates. The primary purpose is to protect from stairs, but a gate can help separate pets or off-limit rooms from the crawling infant.

Parents who practice attachment parenting may avoid anything that "contains" their baby, such as gates, and believe that babies need to be allowed to roam freely within their environment. But many still believe in using gates:

- Babies who are early walkers or very curious, and who have not yet developed the skill to listen or stop when you ask, may need a gate for safety.

- Gate use will really depend entirely on the floor plan and the placement of stairs, etc..

- You can have gates wherever you feel you need them in your house.
  - Some are extra-long to provide room separation.
  - They can help keep pets and children apart.

Things They Wear Now

Stores are stacked with baby clothes, and grandma is often asked to knit or to pick up something special if on vacation, so you need to know a bit about clothing.

Quilts and Blankets

Newborn babies conjure romantic notions of heirloom quilts. My grandsons received some beautiful handmade quilts, and I made some, too for the first one, but quilts are now considered a smothering hazard for sleeping babies.

- Quilts can be used for tummy time as long as someone is with the baby.

- If blankets are used instead of quilts, they are hand-knit, preferably with natural fibers.

- If you haven't knit or crocheted for a while, it might be a good time to get back at it. If you don't know how, it's a good excuse to learn. Most yarn shops give some lessons, and you can keep it simple. The nice thing is your grandchild will have an heirloom made by you.

> *A blanket I made my grandson out of a bulk-department-store yarn pilled. At an early age, my grandson was able to pull off little chunks and put them in his mouth! After all the effort to make it for him, we threw it out.*

> *Many baby blankets and baby toys have 'tabs' of fabric/ribbon on them—babies like to feel them.*
>
> *Not knowing this, my daughter and I removed them from a gift my grandson received.*

— I kept the blanket I knit to bring my children home from the hospital. It is my now grandson's favorite. As he got older he used it as a 'pillow'. Toddlers don't use pillows, but as this has a very loose pattern, it is fine to fold it for him to use this way.

- Try making one out of soft cotton yarn or good-quality baby yarn.

- Do not put fringes or buttons and bows on the blanket.

Baby Swaddling

There are a few different camps on swaddling. It has come and gone in fashion over the years. Some people believe that swaddling is constrictive to baby movement and can lead to over-heating, particularly if you swaddle very tightly or keep the baby's arms in. Others swear by the soothing, calming effect of swaddling.

> You may or may not have swaddled your baby; it seems to come and go in fashion.
>
> It is the most frequent thing I am asked to teach parents.

I am in the swaddling camp for the young baby. They seem to like the sensation and most really do settle well. A swaddled baby is a lovely, snuggly little baby package that is easy to carry around in the football hold, but it also assures that the baby stays on her back for sleep. If over-heating is a concern, you can get muslin cotton, not put so many clothes on baby, and put no blanket on top.

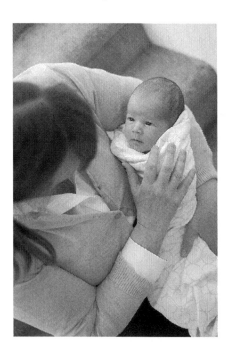

Most young babies like to be swaddled, but not too tightly—just enough for them to feel secure.

- It isn't hard, but it takes some practice to have the baby neatly swaddled—not that neatness counts.

- You want the baby to feel secure, but tight swaddling that keeps the legs very straight is associated with hip problems.

- There are many sites showing how to swaddle. This is a very simple one to follow: http://www.youtube.com/watch?v=PnJ7ykXDpDA

- The baby will let you know when she no longer wants to be swaddled; she will resist and squirm rather than snuggle in.

- Some babies like their arms out, particularly as they get older, but they may not settle as well then.

Receiving Blankets

To swaddle, you need a receiving blanket, but most store bought ones are small and rectangular rather than square. This makes it hard to swaddle the baby properly. Instead, if you sew, you can have fun making some receiving blankets.

> I replaced my fifty-year-old Singer with a new sewing machine, just to be able to make large, square receiving blankets and burping cloths for my grandson!
>
> They were so popular that some of my daughter's friends asked if I would make them for their babies.

- There are wonderful printed materials in flannel, muslin, or other light cotton for warmer climates.

- Edge a forty-five-inch-width of material, squared for the best results.

Baby Wearing

For those of us who used front carriers and backpacks (we called them "snugglis"), the advantages of wearing your baby are well known. We did the laundry, made dinner, and were able to attend to our baby immediately. Some colicky babies respond really well to being 'worn', the movement and snuggled sensation seems to soothe them. As you might expect, there is a much greater selection of ways to "wear" a baby now, and there is a lot of emphasis on slings as well as carriers.

- Some brands of slings (with elastic in the front) have been linked with smothering because the baby can be kept in too tight of a curl.

- Like my grandmother, some women use a long piece of fabric to wrap around themselves, with the baby in the front or back.

The Diaper Bag

The diaper bag is now a fashion accessory, and much deliberation can go into the purchase:

- Some mothers don't want it to look like a bag at all; others wear the diaper bag proudly.

- It is a very personal purchase, and while you might see one you think would be the perfect gift, resist the urge to buy without the mother seeing it. Buy her a gift card instead.

- A good bag will have many different compartments, suitable for easy access to cell phones, wallets, and sippy cups or bottles. They also have handles and straps for carrying and large clips for hanging on strollers.

Lug makes very sturdy and attractive bags that are useful for diapers, among other things. After two years, my daughter's diaper bag looks like new, and in brown, it shows no dirt, and her husband isn't embarrassed to use it. They are popular for resale or for continued use for the gym when the baby's diaper days are done.

Clothing

One night at a friend's house, we were talking about a trendy children's clothing chain that had recently opened a store in our community. One grandfather who had been in sales piped up: "You grandmothers are the demographic they are after. They know you have the money and time to shop and can't resist having your grandchild in all the latest styles." He was right. I ventured to this store immediately after hearing about it. Everyone there was my age, and most were talking on their cell phones to their children, wanting to know the sizes of grandchildren for items they had in their hands. I smiled. It was like a grandmother's heaven.

I struggled at first with newborns wearing brown, black, or fatigue prints, but I have gotten over it because they are usually paired with another milder color and are often so cute. Many of the major high-end stores also have fabulous baby sections where sleepers can cost much more than what you will pay at other stores. They may have cuter prints, but sometimes they have odd little openings on the sides, which make changing difficult. Often, quantity is more important in sleepers and t-shirts, especially in

> **You can't rely on baby clothes to fit the age they claim.**
>
> *Both of my grandsons were in six-month size clothes at two months of age, and neither was more than the 50th percentile for size.*
>
> **Get gift receipts!**

those early days of frequent changes, so a five-pack of cheaper, but decent sleepers may be more appreciated than one expensive one!

"Onesies" or "bodysuits" are odd words that you will hear often, and you will likely end up buying a few of them. It refers to cozy little one-piece cotton underwear that babies wear over their diapers and sometimes under their clothes or as clothes. It's like a sleeper with the legs cut off and a t-shirt on top, usually with no snaps down the front. Instead, they have snaps in the crotch for diaper changes and sometimes have long, short, or no sleeves. They can have very cute logos or designs and are like the t-shirt of the baby crowd.

Toys and Play

There are many, many different toys out there, for every age, interest, and pocketbook. Your children's favorite toys may or may not be available now, or there might be improved versions.

One of the leading toy companies came out with retro toys, bringing back toys that you might recognize. I did buy my grandson the telephone. I wasn't sure he would understand what it was because it doesn't look like the phones do today, but it was one of my children's' favorite toys, so I bought it as a sentimental gesture. He loves it, and amazingly, he picked up the receiver as though he had seen it used every day!

> A sage grandmother told me, *"Play has become adult driven. The world is perceived as a very scary place, and children must first be safe and then organized, although I see this as a sad change—it is far out of my control—when my grandbabies are with me, we do lots of 'old school' activities. The babies spend more time being held while we play and when we eat. Just spending time together with different ages works well, remembering that the littlest one gets the first pick."*

Tempting as it may be, it's not up to you to buy all the big, fancy toys. One friend was quick to tell me that the parents are Santa Claus, not the grandparents. I am glad she reminded me of this because my mother insisted on being Santa to my children and wanted to be the one to buy "the present" under the tree. This was odd because we weren't often together at Christmas for her to enjoy their pleasure in opening her gifts. I must admit, it was handy at times when particular toys were in popular demand and I couldn't get locally, e.g., Cabbage Patch dolls. But, I didn't felt good about her being the center of this process.

Here is what other grandmas suggest you think about before you buy a certain present:

- Ask if you can buy it, and listen if they say no.

> One mother of two advises, *"Avoid buying very noisy toys. Do you really want the parents associating an annoying sound with you?"*

- The child doesn't get the toy until the parents can or want to buy it for her.

- You can offer to give the parents the money to buy the gift when they choose.

- Ask if there is anything else, you can buy for the child.

Your child may have said it is fine for you to buy a certain toy for your grandchild, or he or she may not want you to, so be ready for the reply. In addition, if you have asked and are given the OK to get an item, you need to know the safety facts.

- Do your best to get good quality, non-toxic toys.

  — Be alert for press releases about toy recalls because of lead paint or faulty mechanisms, even by the most reputable manufacturers.

> **Most toys have recommended age ranges:**
>
> *Follow their suggestions, unlike clothing they appear to be accurate.*

Various organizations give ratings on toys each year:

- In the United States, try http://www.cpsc.gov/.

- In Canada, try http://www.hc-sc.gc.ca/cps-spc/pubs/cons/toy_safe-jouet_secur-eng.php.

Play has become serious business for some parents; focused on learning and bettering the child rather than just fun. This can be your role: plain old fun. Pat-a-Cake and I'm a Little Teapot—are easy to play and bring a big smile or giggle your way, even if you get it mixed up! I couldn't remember all the words at first and had to rely on books and CDs to sing along to. After a while, I was surprised at how easy they are to remember. There are many benefits to child development of rhyme and musical rhythm. I find the time at music group with my grandson to be relaxing and rewarding to us both.

At Your House

You may want to have some equipment and toys to be able to provide proper care for your grandchild:

- As tempted as you are, try not to buy baby equipment from garage sales or off websites unless you know the brand and features of the item. First, determine if the parents even want it.

- Car seats, cribs, etc., have safety standards that change.

— You cannot be assured of the safety of secondhand items; parts may be broken or missing.

— If you do buy something inappropriate, the parents may just throw it away.

— Plus, you will not seem informed or up-to-date in your grandparent knowledge.

- If you see something of interest, you can always check for recalls and safety warnings online, and ask your child about buying the particular item.

    — For example, the Nap Nanny baby seat was connected to child deaths and was recalled, but the garage sale sellers might not realize that.

Keep some toys at your house for all the children to use. Just make sure they are safe and stored in a safe place.

10. Parenting Today

Changes in infant feeding and strollers are minor in the impact they can have on the grandparent/child relationship compared to issues over child rearing and discipline. The way your child chooses to parent may surprise you. It can reflect the differences between the generations about the best way to raise baby.

It will help you to know some of the things this mother is talking about because your child and partner may have decided to adopt some of these parenting options and you will be expected to support their efforts.

One very smart young mother of two told me, *"From attachment parenting to Ferberizing to the Weissbluth method to helicopter parenting to being a tiger mom and reading books like Nurtureshock, there are so many things to either enforce that what we're doing as parents is right or wrong. It's hard to keep up. My mom said that when she was raising us, she just did what she felt was right. I think that we are losing some of that 'feeling' in parenting (or just trusting your gut) in favor of different theories or practices. She told me, 'Don't read all of this stuff; just do what you think is right.' I really appreciated her perspective."*

Attachment parenting, Ferberizing, CIO, the Weissbluth method (sleep training) are discussed in more detail elsewhere in the book (See Index). Here is a primer on two other important terms now:

Helicopter parenting or over-parenting: Like helicopters, these parents hover above their children, especially in their schooling and other life activities. Helicopter parenting was identified in the 1960s, so you may have been raised that way or practiced it yourself, but it has come to the forefront in the past ten years.

> Helicopter parents can grow into helicopter grandparents— who intrude in their grandfamily's life.

Tiger mom: This term was popularized in Amy Chau's book, '*Battle Hymn of the Tiger Mother*.' Chau is a Chinese American mother of two girls. Although a mother of any culture or ethnicity can be traditional and strict, tiger moms are also called "Chinese mothers." I knew a Chinese family in which the son practiced his math between courses in restaurants. That was more of a tiger father situation, but that boy has grown up to be a very social-adapted, polite, and academically accomplished young man. Many experts believe that tiger parenting exerts too much pressure on children.

ATTACHMENT PARENTING

Attachment parenting (AP) is one of the biggest areas of change and controversy in childcare. If your child practices AP, you will need to know more about it because it can affect your role as a grandparent.

Attachment parenting stresses the importance of proximity, protection, and predictability for a baby. Parents are encouraged to practice the seven attachment tools, or the "Baby B's". Although the creators don't want us to view these as a list, it is impossible not to. Here are the components:

Birth Bonding: Birth should be as intervention-free and medication-free as possible to promote bonding with the baby. There is acknowledgment that bonding with the baby can take time.

Breast-Feeding: Breastfeeding is the optimal way to feed an infant. AP also promotes breastfeeding as a way for mothers to read their baby's cues and body language, which encourage bonding.

Baby Wearing: Baby wearing in slings or carriers is promoted to improve closeness and bonding but also for the baby to learn about her environment. A baby learns a lot in the arms of a busy caregiver; she is listening as the mother talks or sings and can feel her heartbeat.

Bedding Close to Baby: AP advocates promote co-sleeping and bed-sharing with infants in touching proximity of the parents.

Belief in the Language Value of Baby's Cry: AP involves responding sensitively to the baby's cries. Babies will develop trust that their caregivers will respond to their needs. Parents gain confidence in their ability to meet their baby's needs. Young babies cry to communicate, not to manipulate. AP parents do not believe in letting the baby cry it out (CIO).

Beware of Baby Trainers: "Baby trainers" are those parents who follow schedules and rules. AP philosophy calls this "convenience parenting," which provides a short-term gain for a long-term loss, and claims that more restrictive parenting approaches create a distance between parents and the baby.

Balance: Fortunately, AP also encourages parents not to neglect the needs of the mother and the couple. This is where being a non-intrusive grandparent is going to have benefits. You will be available if they ask for help.

Attachment Parenting in Practice

Parents follow AP to different degrees, as much as they can or want to. Some parents start out wanting to practice AP fully, but may find it too intense and choose to use those parts that make them comfortable. There may be some guilt if parents felt this was the very best way to raise their baby and they have somehow failed, but parents need to do what is best for them and the baby at the time.

> One mother told me, *"I practiced some elements of attachment parenting; I know my dad didn't agree with it. He would say that we were 'too attentive' and needed to make Liam more independent. I told him it wasn't a fair comment to a working mother. If I wasn't around Liam for the most of the day, I certainly wasn't going to ignore him or try to make him more independent when I was home. Now that he's older, I realize how much easier he is to discipline than other kids who are not as attached. That is the biggest piece that my dad and I disagree. But now he says what great parents we are and what a great child we have, so although he won't admit it, he realizes that what we did worked for us and worked for the type of child we have."*

Baby Sign Language

Yes, you read that right—baby sign language! Baby sign language is intended to help babies who cannot speak yet (making them preverbal) to communicate their needs. It is believed that babies can start to understand the signs at around six months and can respond with their own signing at around ten months. Rather than an official sign language such as American Sign Language (ASL), babies are taught gestures to represent their needs rather than learn signs for actual letters or words.

Babies who can't express what they want (a certain toy or a banana), will likely scream loudly and cause frustration for everyone around them, particularly non-parents. So teaching them another way to tell you their needs bridges the gap.

Baby signing is thought to increase cognitive development and expressive language, but some experts worry that signing will decrease verbal language development because they may sign rather than talk as they mature.

> One-year-olds often point to items they want or like before they develop the vocabulary to express their needs.
>
> *My grandson developed his own "sign". He would take our finger and lead us to what he wanted, before he could tell us in words.*

As expected, a number of companies have designed programs with specific signs depicted in DVDs, flashcards, wall charts, etc.. Like all new skills, it takes patience and repetition, but babies seem to enjoy signing.

One woman I know used signing with her third child for a few key words related to her favorite toys and food items. She didn't follow a program; rather, she just taught the baby a few signs. It helped lessen her baby's and everyone else's frustration and considerably decreased what she described as intolerable (and exhausting) screeching, making for a happier family all around. You will definitely want to learn the signs your grandbaby knows so that you can communicate well.

Behavior

Stranger Anxiety and Separation Anxiety

You may have been there from the moment the baby was born; and therefore, feel that you know the baby as well as possible. However, you probably aren't there all the time, or you may have been there only on holidays, and your grandchild might experience stranger anxiety and/or separation anxiety with you. Because both of these cause distress for the baby (and her parents) and it is very likely that she will cry, be prepared in case it happens to you. If you keep in contact, the stranger anxiety will be minimized; it is temporary.

> Be patient. With increased contact and as the baby gets older, she will soon recognize that you are her grandma, and all will be well.
>
> *Keeping contact over the Internet may help prevent stranger anxiety.*

I remember the first time my parents visited us after my son was born. They were so very excited to see my six-month-old son that my mother rushed across the airport, grabbing him out of my arms to hug him. Apart from our short visit when he was a newborn, they hadn't met each other. Consequently, he was terrified of someone who was really a stranger to him. He cried and cried. She was hurt. But, he was behaving as expected for a baby of his age. She would have been much better to approach him slowly and let him get used to her, but she was too overcome with joy to see him to wait.

Stranger anxiety: This is one of the first emotional milestones a baby experiences. It is normal for babies to have stranger anxiety around six to twelve months. It is a positive sign that the baby recognizes an unfamiliar situation or person and looks to the parents for comfort or to leave the unsettling situation. The baby might withdraw, look away, cry, or cling to her parents.

Separation anxiety: This is also a healthy emotional milestone. A baby is attached to her mother and father, and when they leave the baby, she gets anxious and cries. If you are the one babysitting and your grandchild starts crying hard when your daughter leaves for a short appointment, you may feel slighted; however, realize this is normal behavior. Try waving bye-bye and distract your grandchild with a toy or a snack.

We expect that a healthy child will outgrow stranger and separation anxiety by age two. If she does not, perhaps there is more going on? I was stunned a few years ago to hear a psychiatrist talk about treating infant mental health problems in her practice. It was hard for me to believe that a baby could have problems that would require mental health care, but it is being identified and happening more and more. The focus is on the parents (or other caregivers) and the baby, and the goal is to promote attachment and communication between them.

Meltdowns and the Terrible Twos

A meltdown is what we called a temper tantrum. Contrary to the title, the "terrible twos" can start when the child is one and last beyond the second year. Meltdowns usually happen when the child cannot voice her needs or understand why she cannot have something. Those parents true to attachment theory will not discipline, hit, ignore, or even do time outs; rather, they try to understand the cause of the meltdown and show the child compassion and love. This is thought to ease the child's anxiety and lessen outbursts.

Diversions often work the best, warm baths with lavender baby wash can be calming. Don't put a thrashing baby in a tub or in a crib alone. Maybe a walk outside or some music can help distract from the toddler's distress.

You will need to be aware of what the parents do or ask them how they want you to respond if there is a meltdown on your watch.

> Children who have frequent or severe temper tantrums, and who cannot be subdued or calm themselves may have psychological problems that a doctor may be able to help with.

Discipline

You were in charge of the family for many years, but now who is the boss? Simple: The parents are. They are charged with setting the rules for how their child is raised and the consequences when they are not followed.

> An otherwise mild-mannered young woman said, "Your child is the boss of their child, so follow their rules. You had your turn." Ouch! She is right, we had our turn.

While you can help teach and enforce the rules, you are not there to create them or to set the moral compass.

One woman who is enjoying her life as a grandparent describes her unique way of managing challenging behavior in her young grandchildren. She is clear that the parents are the bosses and uses this to her advantage. Instead of being angry at minor misbehavior, she pretends to be worried about the "bosses" being mad at them both, and suddenly the child comes onto her side, wants to help her, and fixes whatever the behavior or problem is.

She explained that while she changed the one-year-old grandson's diaper, his three-year-old sister found a crayon and colored on the wall. She noticed this and exclaimed, "Oh, Ava, I am going to be in so much trouble with your mom. This is her wall, and we aren't supposed to color on it. Can you help me fix it?" Ava grabbed a cloth and cleanser and scrubbed away busily until the marks were gone. Grandma remains her best friend, the marks are gone, and everyone is happy.

> An experienced mother told me, *"If the child's life isn't in danger, then the grandmother should likely stay out of it,"*

But as effective as this may seem in the short term to get some cooperation, I suggest you never blame the parents or do anything to make them look bad.

One grandmother I know has an annoying habit of dismissing the parents' wishes by saying, "Your mommy won't let you (or me) do that," implying that the child could do something fun or eat something special if not for the parents. This makes the parents the bad guys, not a good thing ever. It also doesn't instill faith in the parents

> One young mother told me that the most annoying behavior of her parents was feeling judged about how she disciplined her baby. *"I think sometimes (actually I know) that grandparents forget what it's like to have a new baby. When my baby first started to assert her independence (as all babies do and what I've come to understand as normal and a good thing), my parents would always make comments like 'Oh, when you guys were little, you never did that.' I found that challenging and irritating to hear because I knew it wasn't true, and it made me feel like they thought it was something that I was doing wrong."*

regarding what happens with this grandmother and the child when the parents aren't there.

A grandmother's role is to support your child to be a good parent. The best route likely would be to try your best to follow what the parents have determined their child is allowed to do, and apologize if things don't go quite as hoped.

Not worrying about being the disciplinarian can take the pressure off and let you have fun being the grandparent you hope to be. However, a friend found out how difficult it can be to grandparent if you fear a child's life is in danger. His little grandson, Josh was playing outside at their house, which is on a busy street. Josh started toward the traffic, Grandpa went after him, and Josh thought he was playing and ran faster right into the street. Grandpa was on autopilot. When he grabbed Josh, he smacked him on the bottom without thinking. He regretted his action greatly and his daughter-in-law was very angry with both of them.

Try to remember that the parents are doing the best they know how. Things have changed and our job is to understand and support them. We won't always do things perfectly, but we can try to follow what they ask of us.

> *If you interfere or make your child feel badly about their parenting, you may find yourself not welcome in their home, damage the relationship with your child, and miss precious time with your grandfamily.*

11. GRANDMOTHER CHALLENGES TODAY

There are many challenges, beyond in-laws, equipment, and infant feeding that can stress the new grandmother. This includes situations such as, when you live far away, boomerang children, adoption, or when something happens with the baby.

GRANDPARENTING FROM A DISTANCE

It's very hard to be far apart from your grandchild. Grandparents today have a distinct advantage over ours—the computer. If you own a computer, it's time to learn about live video chat or a voice over Internet Protocol (VoiP) program. If you don't have a computer, it is time to get one so that you can enjoy real-time communication with your little ones.

> *Don't forget to send pictures of yourself and your husband, pets, etc., to your grandchild, and as she gets older, tell her little stories in letters or messages just for her.*

- Skype is live, free communication with people anywhere in the world. My friend has talked to her grandchildren regularly since they were born. Soon enough, even your youngest grandchildren will be going to the computer and wanting to talk to you, like hers do. To register, go to http://www.skype.com/intl/en-us/home.

- Facetime is also live and free. It is video conferencing software used on products like iPad or iPhone.

One friend used most of her holiday time from work to visit her grandchildren; now that the children are older, the parents use this as time for them to vacation. This allows the grandparents to care for the children and enjoy taking them to their school and sports activities. They also holiday as one large group, which is a treat for everyone.

> If you are not invited or not comfortable to stay at your grandfamily's home, try a bed & breakfast close to their house.
>
> This way you can visit for shorter periods throughout your stay. It may reduce stress that can arise from being in close surroundings for prolonged periods.

One smart long distance grandmother found a way to use her spare grandmother time (time she thought she would have spent with her grandchildren had they lived close by). She makes bags that are sold to raise money for the *Grandmothers to Grandmothers Campaign* in African countries. She loves to sew and knows that her work is supporting grandmothers who are raising their grandchildren alone. There can also be opportunities for grandmothers to share some grandma time through volunteer 'snuggle' or cradling programs in children's hospitals or crisis shelters.

THE SINGLE PARENT AND BOOMERANG CHILDREN

Not all single parents move home and not all boomerang children (adult children who come and go from their parent's home, with or without partners) have children. There are so many different combinations of families that fall within this range, I have combined them.

More women have babies without partners now,

> One thirty-something boomerang daughter moved in with her parents when her baby was born. Despite the adjustments at first, they loved having them there. The grandparents were devastated was when her maternity leave was over and she and the baby returned to a city almost twelve hour drive away. They have learned to Skype and since they retired, they can visit often.

or sometimes their relationship is such that they choose to parent alone. Your child may not have left home yet, or you may be (re)opening your home to parent(s) and baby. Some boomerang children stay for a short time, others for years (and years). Having such a close family can be a wonderful experience for everyone. It can give your life renewed purpose; keep you very active and involved. You and your grandchild get the day-to-day love in your life. And, research has shown that a child raised in a multi-generational family can experience much love, support, and continuity in their day-to-day lives.

What if you just remarried, downsized, or just started your retirement with plans of travel or a calm life of art lessons and lunch with your friends? Suddenly everything is up in the air. If your grandfamily lives with you for any length of time, you it will require adjustments of space, communication, roles, and resources. The dynamics will change, drastically once baby comes along. The single mother may need more support and physical help with baby care, but may feel she has to do it alone or the opposite and leave much to grandma to do. Ground rules with clear boundaries, are needed by all-round (in any situation). Finances may or may not be an issue for you. You don't want to become a fulltime babysitter, yet be as supportive as possible especially if her circumstances are stressful to her.

As always, recognize that if there has been a history of communication problems, they may escalate with stressors like cohabitating and babies and boomerang. For example, triangulation, where one family member won't communicate directly with another, but will talk to another member may be more pronounced with more and new people in the house and will be very perplexing to someone new to this dynamic. You have a long history with at least one of the people and are learning with the new baby or partner. You will all have to work at this new arrangement, but I have seen it work well when people do.

DIVORCE AND GRANDPARENT RIGHTS

Divorce happens. Usually custody is shared, and in that case, you can expect to have some access to your grandchild. However, if the divorce is hostile, you may find yourself in a position of being related to the non-custodial parent, and that may be very difficult. One woman I know had a better relationship with her ex-in-laws than her ex-husband so that did not affect the grandparent's ability to see the children.

In a rare situation, both parents may decide that a grandparent cannot spend time with her grandchild. The law related to grandparent access and custody varies, but there is something in each jurisdiction to ensure that in cases of marriage breakdown or death that you can fight for access to your grandchild. Less common are situations in which the grandparents must step in take over the raising of their grandchildren. This is important with many needs that are beyond the scope of this book

> One grandma was upset that her son and his wife had separated. His wife moved 100 miles away. *"He has time with Jade every other weekend; he brings her home to his little apartment. I know his time with her is precious. He is good about us spending time with her when she is here, but I always wait for an invitation. It is sad for us, but it's all we have for now."*

ADOPTION

Adoption is more complicated now; babies are rarely adopted anonymously, with open (everyone knowing who is who) or international adoptions more the norm. There is no question that you will be grandmother to any new addition to your grandfamily. Often parents adopt after years of fertility failures and financial burden.

Birth parents provide health information for adoption files, but as children start having their own children, they may want more information about or want to meet their birth family. One woman I know became a grandmother when the daughter she had given up for adoption thirty-two years earlier made contact with her for the first time. Suddenly, she had a two-year-old grandson and another grandbaby on the way. She was shy and overwhelmed at first, but once meeting them, she was as proud as any grandma I have met. She was invited to family occasions, and gradually became a member of this loving extended family. Her life is special because of this grandmother role, one that she had never expected.

WHEN THINGS DON'T TURN OUT AS PLANNED

We tend to idolize babies, but around four percent of babies are born with some type of congenital anomaly. "Congenital" means that the problem occurs before or early after birth. Anomalies, also known as malformations, defects, abnormalities, or deformities can range from fatal heart defects where parts of the heart do not develop to large birthmarks.

There are too many problems to list, but they can be caused by chromosomal abnormalities (e.g., Down syndrome), genetics (e.g., cystic fibrosis), environment (e.g., fetal alcohol syndrome, caused by the mother ingesting excessive alcohol), or a teratogen (a drug or other agent, e.g., thalidomide or German measles). Sometimes they occur spontaneously, with no known cause.

If the baby has a problem, it may be obvious at birth (or before, during an ultrasound), or it may not become apparent until later. If one problem is noted, sometimes the doctor will look for other problems. For example, if a baby has only two vessels in the cord (rather than three), this is thought to indicate a problem with the kidneys or heart, and the baby will likely have these organs checked by ultrasound.

One thing is certain: If the baby has a problem, the entire family will be affected. There can be myriad of emotions: shock, pain, guilt, anger, disappointment, worry about stigma, and shame, to name a few.

> Many, including grandma, grieve the loss of the ideal baby and the dreams they had for their life together.

While some may think it ruins the pregnancy experience to know there is a problem beforehand, it is best to know. The parents can prepare for medical treatment or extra attendants at the birth, and it gives the parents time to adjust. I have seen parents go through hell in the delivery room when a baby was born with an unexpected anomaly and seen parents be relieved when an anticipated problem was not as severe as they had envisioned.

How to help

This is a very stressful time; you can help by:

- Letting the parents vent. Listen. Listen. Listen.

- Try to avoid judgement in your words or actions.

- Help to alleviate their guilt if they express it.

- Become informed about the problem and understand what it might mean for the baby and family (surgery or other treatments).

- Do what you can to lighten their burden (housework, caring for other children).

THE WORST CAN HAPPEN

Being around mothers and their babies can be the most wonderful experience in the world. I am so grateful for sharing birth with so many women, but when a mother loses a baby to miscarriage or stillbirth or the death of a child at any time, it is the most tragic situation. I have held the hands of many mothers who have experienced the loss of their babies and cried with them when the worst has happened in the delivery room.

Fetal death, which refers to a baby who dies in the uterus or is born dead after twenty weeks' gestation or over 12–18 ounces (350–500 grams, depending on where you live) is considered stillborn. Before that time, a fetal loss is called a miscarriage or spontaneous abortion.

A stillbirth usually requires special paperwork such as birth and death certificates, which can be stressful for the parent. Parents may want to stay with their baby after she has died; most units have a quiet room for families to spend time with the baby. Many units have bassinettes and clothing for picture taking. Some parents may take the baby home with them for a period or to a funeral home.

Grief

This is all very likely new to the parents, and how things are handled around them and how they perceive their pregnancy will influence their response. For some, the baby is a person from conception, while for others they do not attach until the mother feels it move, and for others, it might not be a person until the baby is born. Each parent might have a different perception on this, and might not be aware until the pregnancy is lost.

> One thing that people said to me after my son died that brought momentary relief was, "If I could take away your pain, I would."
>
> Somehow, these words allowed me to release some of the agony for just an instant.

If the baby dies before or just after birth, the mother's body is still postpartum with all the same hormonal changes and physical adjustments. Her body needs to adjust and heal like any new mother. Her breasts may leak milk and become engorged, another symbol of her loss, and her loose abdomen will be an ongoing reminder that they have lost their baby.

Women are often put on other hospital units after the birth with nurses who do not know how to care for them, or if they are very sick, they may still be on the labor unit hearing other babies being born and happy families. Their pain is deep, and many things can trigger grief.

> If you have the opportunity, extend a hug to your child.
>
> The most important thing is your support and love.

The woman may be on maternity leave but not have a baby, and her partner will likely go back to work after a short time. This is a potentially bleak and lonely time for the woman, and if you can find the time to be with her, please do so. Even just sitting quietly, making tea, and letting her vent her feelings (as much as she needs to) or just being quiet are helpful.

Grief can trigger past losses that people may not be aware of or had thought were resolved. If you have experienced the loss of a baby or child, this could be a very difficult time for you.

Losing my first pregnancy to miscarriage at thirteen weeks and then experiencing the death of my son when he was fourteen years old, I can say there was no comparison to the impact of both of these losses in my world.

At the time, the miscarriage was the most momentous event that I had ever experienced. I was far away from my husband and parents. It was a lonely and sad time. I felt empty and defeated. I can say now that what I badly needed right then was a warm hug.

Grief.com is a site by the grandson of Elizabeth Kubler Ross, who was famous for identifying the stages of grief (denial, anger, bargaining, depression, and acceptance). It has a list of the best and worst things to say to a grieving person. You may want to look at these if there is a need in your life: http://grief.com/helpful-tips/the-10-best-and-worst-things-to-say-to-someone-in-grief/

> I got momentary relief from grief when people told me, "If this can happen to you, it can happen to anyone."
>
> It may help the couple who did everything 'correct' in the pregnancy and are now blaming themselves unnecessarily.

For a young family, dealing with death and funerals may be a new experience:

- Parents need to decide how they want to handle things that they may not have any experience with, such as planning a burial or cremation.
  - Much may depend on the baby's age and circumstances of the loss.
  - Your job is to support and help them with this very difficult decision.
  - There may be a family plot you can offer them.
- Funerals are an expense new parents do not anticipate.
  - If you can help with funeral costs, this may ease their stress.
- Some communities have individual and group support for families who have experienced perinatal or pregnancy loss.
  - Try to find out what is available in your community.

— Compassionate Friends provides peer support to families who have lost a child. They may be able to help the parents cope with their pain better than someone who has not experienced such loss will be able to do. http://www.compassionatefriends.org/home.aspx.

What about You?

Everyone needs time to heal. This includes the grandparents. You may have known the gender or name of the baby, bought gifts, and fantasized about how you would grandparent her. You need to be there for the parents, but also take care of yourself:

> If you had a similar loss, you can share that you have gone through some of the same feelings and say you are there to support them.
>
> Do not to overshadow or diminish the parents' experience or burden them with your own grief.

- Talk to your partner, a good friend, or spiritual advisor.

  — If your distress is unbearable (can't sleep, eat, or cope with daily life), talk to a health professional.

- This may be a good time to help the parents with meals, laundry, and other chores.

  — It can keep you busy and feeling focused during this awful time.

- Avoid any sudden decisions or judgments.

  — It's likely not a good time to move away or go on vacation unless you had already planned it, and if you can postpone it, do so.

If your friends have experienced a loss in their grandfamily, acknowledge their loss as you would any other member of the family, with a card and meal or a donation to an organization associated with the parents or a condition of the child.

What If You Aren't Enjoying Being a Grandmother?

There will be times when being a grandmother isn't all you hoped it would be. Life can offer challenges, and the larger your family becomes, the more likely it is that there will be disappointments and tragedies. The idealization of grandmother may make it harder for you to accept things aren't what you expected.

What If You Don't Like Babies?

One woman, who was always very kind to me, hated babies. She loved every form of animal life, but when it came to human babies, she said that she could not stand them, and she would appear physically repulsed at the mention of babies. She had a child, by adoption; she told me her husband had brought the child home, so she felt she had to keep him. I met them when he was an adult, and I saw a loving relationship between them. I could tell that she was very interested in and cared for her grandchildren by him, but they were grown when I met them. When I asked her how she handled them as babies, she said she just did what was necessary, but as they got older, her love for them grew, as it had with her son.

> Children aren't babies forever, and soon they are smiling and cooing, so rest easy if you aren't immediately 'in-love' your new grandbaby.

Not Feeling Appreciated

Just as the love for your children knows no boundaries, chances are neither does the love for your grandchildren. But, even that love can be tested. Not all babies are easy to settle; some do not snuggle as you had hoped. You may go home feeling empty and used, rather than loved and appreciated after a day of diaper changes, cooking, cleaning, and post-partum emotions.

If that happens, look inward:

- Were you just feeling sensitive?

- Are you all just plain exhausted?

- Things will likely look and feel better after a good night's sleep!

Try to remember that when arguments happen, it can affect not just those in the fight, but everyone around them. Recent research has shown that yelling around children can leave them feeling unsettled and unsafe and lead to anger problems later in life. I notice that my grandson even reacts to people arguing on TV. Young children do not understand the context or likely even the words, so your arguing over a recipe or the date when someone's aunt got married could be threatening enough to upset them.

The baby starts crying and the parents get upset. They get anxious, and then the baby cries more. They leave or you leave if it's their house. No one feels good. Perhaps we should always behave as though we might make the baby cry and watch what we say all of the time!

TODAY'S GRANDMOTHER GOES FORTH GENTLY

Now you are up-to-date about pregnancy, birth, and baby; please remember to learn about your child's preferred method of parenting, follow that as closely as you can, and go forth very softly with your newfound knowledge.

Be mindful of your words, your tone, your actions, and your intention. Are you supporting your new grand-family or needing to be right?

It might be helpful to think that everyone tries to do a good job with parenting and grandparenting; it isn't always easy. Your children will un-

> One happy grandmother of seven grandchildren and step-grandchildren told me, "As grandparents, we can continue to speak under our breath: 'How ever did you manage to grow up?' But keep that to yourself."

doubtedly make mistakes as you did and will, but we can help them in their journey.

Being a grandmother today might not always be easy, and you won't always be a perfect grandparent. Likely, your child will be forgiving of little indiscretions if he or she knows that you are well meaning and trying to be a helpful, loving grandmother who is invested in their wellbeing.

> **One friend summarized many of my thoughts this way:** *"The most important thing for a grandparent to learn—if you have a good relationship with your kids—is it will continue, in spite of raging hormones, sleep deprivation, body issues, baby issues (colic, etc.), organization, or lack thereof. All issues can and will be weathered.*
>
> *However, if the pre-baby relationship has been rocky, you might be well to prepare for some big storms or extended silent treatment. Against all our hopes, babies can cause more stress on family relationships, not less. We must work to be supportive grandmothers and families."*

I have tried my best to prepare you to be a modern, informed, *Today's Grandmother*, one who is active and engaged in her grandfamily's life.

Remember to Ask. Ask. Ask.... And listen. Listen. Listen.

Be mindful, self-affirming, and take care of yourself.

The last words go to a wise young woman I have known since she was ten years old. She is a wonderful mother to her three-year-old daughter and one-year-old son: "Enjoy the baby.... I think if the focus of the grandparents is on the baby and on getting joy out of this new being, then it will form the basis of this new relationship (i.e., baby, grandparents, and parents) and only happiness will ensue."

12. TODAY'S RESOURCES

I have tried to cover all the questions and situations you may encounter. If you have concerns about things you see happening with your grandchild, don't assume that what the parents are doing is wrong; remember, it just may be different from how you raised them.

You can get handouts and brochures at your public health or doctor's offices. The parents are likely getting their information online. There are many parenting and baby websites available out there, but how can you be sure they are reliable? You need to know the major sites that may be informing your child's parenting practices and your grandchild's health, but most importantly, you need to know what knowledge is guiding the health care professionals who are advising your child.

> It is best to do your homework and check first before you challenge how your children are parenting.

Many of the professional sites require registration, login, and password access, but all of the sites I have listed have open public access. That way you can learn what information is accurate and evidence-based in easy-to-understand language.

If there is a conflict between you and your child, perhaps you can use these sites to try to discuss the situation from an unbiased, informed viewpoint. Chances are the parents will have their reasons for what they are doing, so check before you make assumptions or accusations.

PRIVATE OR NON-GOVERNMENTAL ORGANIZATIONS

Many organizations on the Internet are happy to advise anyone who will listen to their views. One grandmother told me that one of her worst fears was her daughter-in-law listening to various online groups about their own versions of proper baby care. The young girl was very influenced by these anonymous opinions, but resisted reading or listening to experienced members of her family.

This list is not exhaustive, but ought to help with questions you may have and you can feel comfortable suggesting them to others:

- Motherisk is an informative site managed by the Hospital for Sick Children and University of Toronto in Toronto, Canada, with trained counselors, researchers, and medical professionals available.

  — They get phone calls from parents and those who care about them and their babies from around the world.

  — They offer studied information online and telephone consultations about medication and other substance use (including hair dye) in pregnancy, and they address the issue of HIV/AIDS. They also have a support and information line that offers guidance and tremendous reassurance for women suffering with nausea and vomiting: http://www.motherisk.org

  — Motherisk hotlines:
    1-877-327-4636 Alcohol and Substance
    1-800-436-8477 Morning Sickness/NVP
    1-888-246-5840 HIV and HIV Treatment
    1-877-439-2744 Motherisk Helpline
    Local number 1-416-813-6780 Motherisk Helpline

- The March of Dimes is an excellent non-profit organization that provides information about pregnancy and baby health, particularly defects, anomalies, and prematurity. The organization advocates for baby health at a governmental level. The US site (http://www.marchofdimes.com) has more educational information than the Canadian site (http://www.marchofdimes.ca), which focuses more on services for the disabled.

- Postpartum Support International (PSI) is an excellent resource that offers support to women struggling with postpartum depression and those who care about them: http://www.postpartum.net

- La Leche League (LLL) has been helping mothers to breastfeed for more than fifty years. It is an international organization with numerous resources in multiple languages and local chapters for peer support: http://www.llli.org/

- Attachment Parenting International is a resource for parents. If your grandfamily is practicing attachment parenting, the site can help you understand what is happening: http://www.attachmentparenting.org

COMMERCIAL SITES

- Babycenter is a site that offers information about development and all aspects of pregnancy, baby care, and toddler care. There are Canadian and American versions: http://www.babycenter.com or http://www.babycenter.ca.

- Once a parent signs up, she can receive weekly notifications about the expected milestones, activities, etc., so that she can anticipate what behaviors will be coming. They seem to be unbiased and sensible.

  — There aren't many pop-ups, but there are links for purchasing items.

- There is nothing to stop an eager grandparent from signing up to receive the weekly e-mails!

  — You would have to register that you had a baby on a certain day, but especially if your child is receiving them, it can open up lines of communication between the two of you when you are concerned about things.

- *Consumer Reports* is an online and print magazine that provides product information and reviews. Its children's product area is very specific and helpful when you are about to buy a product, particularly one that is secondhand: http://www.consumerreports.org/cro/index.htm

- The Dr. Sears family of physicians and a nurse are seen on TV and have numerous books in publication that many new parents are using as a reference: http://www.askdrsears.com/

- *Happiest Baby on the Block* and *Happiest Toddler on the Block* are very easy-to-read and enjoyable books that detail Dr. Karp's) five S's for baby care: http://www.colichelp.com/shop/happiestbabyontheblock.html

- Penny Simkin is a most wonderfully empathetic physical therapist and doula. Her site offers many birthing resources, particularly comfort measures for the expectant and new parents: http://www.pennysimkin.com/

  — I have heard Penny talk a few times and see how everyone is so energized to provide excellent, woman-directed care from her insights.

  — Her DVDs review the comfort measures with which partners and grandparents can help.

- Kellymom is a breastfeeding/parenting site with lots of common sense information on it: http://kellymom.com/

Government Agencies

Governments are charged with protecting the public. They invest huge amounts of time and money in disease control, health promotion, and education programs. Many local and national organizations have developed wonderfully informative sites for professionals, policy makers, and the public. The main American and Canadian sites are:

- The Centers for Disease Control and Prevention is a US government agency that provides up-to-date information for parents and professionals. The site is arranged alphabetically: http://www.cdc.gov/parents/infants/index.html

- Health Canada offers many sites with information about pregnancy (http://www.hc-sc.gc.ca/hl-vs/preg-gros/index-eng. php) and babies (http://www.hc-sc.gc.ca/hl-vs/babies-bebes/ index-eng.php).

PROFESSIONAL ORGANIZATIONS

The organizations that certify obstetricians, midwives, and pediatricians have evaluated the evidence to provide their members with guidelines for safe practice. These are the major organizations:

- The American Academy of Pediatrics (AAP) is the professional organization providing professional resources for those responsible for the care of children from birth to the end of adolescence: http://www.aap.org/en-us/Pages/Default.aspx.
  - The AAP lay website for the public is excellent. "Healthy Children" is available at: http://www.healthychildren.org/ English/Pages/default.aspx. The site can also help parents find pediatricians in their area.

- The Canadian Pediatric Society (CPS) provides position statements, education, and advocacy for pediatricians and others who provide care for children: http://www.cps.ca/
  - CPS also has a parent site, "Caring for Kids," that is open access: http://www.caringforkids.cps.ca/

- The American Congress of Obstetricians and Gynecologists (ACOG) is the professional association for American obstetricians and gynecologists.

  > SOGC and ACOG also have information about women's health and menopause that might be helpful for your own health questions!

  - ACOG offers clinical guidelines and support to practitioners, as well as information for patients: http://www.acog.org/For_Patients. The site can help patients find obstetricians in their area.

- The Society of Obstetricians and Gynecologists of Canada (SOGC) is the professional association of obstetricians and gynecologist across Canada.

  — SOGC also has a public and professional website that provides evidence-based information: http://www.sogc.org/index_e.asp

- The American College of Nurse-Midwives represents midwives in the US: http://www.midwife.org/

> Look for sites by professional and governmental organizations that have done the research for you.

BIBLIOGRAPHY

- Anomalies/defects: http://www.marchofdimes.com/baby/ birthdefects.html http://www.marchofdimes.ca

- Assisted reproduction: http://www.cdc.gov/art/

- Attachment: Antonucci, T.C., H. Akiyama, and K. Takahashi. "Attachment and Close Relationships across the Life Span." *Attachment & Human Development*. 6 (2004): 353–370.

- Attachment parenting: http://www.attachmentparenting.org/

- Baby-led weaning: http://www.babyledweaning.com/

- BMI: http://www.nhlbi.nih.gov/guidelines/obesity/BMI/bmicalc.htm

- Body mass index: http://nhlbisupport.com/bmi/

- BPA: http://www.sciencedaily.com/releases/2008/01/080130092108.htm

- Brain development and routines: http://www.caringforkids.cps.ca/ handouts/your_babys_brain

- Bumbo seats: http://bumbo.com http://www.bumbocanada.com/ registration.php

- Car seats: http://www.nhtsa.gov/Safety/CPS

- Car seat deaths: http://ca.news.yahoo.com/blogs/dailybrew/ edmonton-child-dies-being-found-overheated-car-185153773.html

- Circumcision: http://pediatrics.aappublications.org/content/early/2012/08/22/peds.2012-1989

- Citronella: www.epa.gov/oppsrrd1/REDs/factsheets/3105fact.pdf

- Colic support, remedies, and information for stressed parents: http://www.colichelp.com/shop/happiestbabyontheblock.html http://pediatrics.aappublications.org/content/116/5/e709.short

- Colic study: http://pediatrics.aappublications.org/content/126/3/e526.long

- Compassionate Friends: http://www.compassionatefriends.org/home.aspx

- Co-sleeping: http://www.cps.ca/english/statements/cp/cp04-02.htm

- Cost of raising a child, 2004: http://www.ccsd.ca/factsheets/family/.

- Cost of raising child: "Expenditures on Children by Families, 2011." US Department of Agriculture, Center for Nutrition Policy and Promotion. Publication Number 1528–2011.

- CPR: http://www.heart.org/HEARTORG/CPRAndECC/CommunityTraining/CommunityProducts/Family-Friendsreg-CPR_UCM_303576_Article.jsp

- Cradle cap: http://www.cpnonline.org/CRS/CRS/pa_cradlcap_hhg.htm

- Dads: Mellor, G., and St. John, W. "Fatigue and work safety behaviour in men during early fatherhood." *American Journal of Men's Health*, 6 (2012), 80-88. http://www.ncbi.nlm.nih.gov/pubmed/21965183

- Diaper services: http://www.diapernet.org/whycloth.htm

- Dylan Viale: http://www.huffingtonpost.com/2012/04/16/dylan-viale_n_1429112.html

- Emotions: Bowen, A., R. Bowen, and N. Muhajarine. "Are Pregnant and Postpartum Women More Moody? Understanding Perinatal

Mood Instability." *Journal of Obstetrics Gynaecology of Canada.* November 2012. http://www.ncbi.nlm.nih.gov/pubmed/23231841

- Epidural: http://www.americanpregnancy.org/labornbirth/epidural.html

- Fetal heart: http://www.babycentre.co.uk/pregnancy/ antenatalhealth/testsandcare/heartbeatowndopplerexpert/

- Financial plans, 529: http://www.savingforcollege.com/intro_ to_529s/name-the-top-7-benefits-of-529-plans.php

- Flathead: Mawji, A, Robinson Vollman, A, Hatfield, J, McNeil, DA, and Sauvé, R. (2013). The Incidence of Positional Plagiocephaly: A Cohort Study. (doi: 10.1542/peds.2012-3438). http://pediatrics. aappublications.org/content/early/2013/07/02/peds.2012-3438. abstract

- Flu shot: http://www.phac-aspc.gc.ca/im/iif-vcg/gs-pg-eng.php#a16

- Folate in food: http://www.phac-aspc.gc.ca/publicat/faaf/chap3-eng.php

- Folic acid: http://www.phac-aspc.gc.ca/fa-af/index-eng.php

- Grandmothers and breastfeeding: de Oliveira, L.D., E. Giugliani, L.C. do Espirito Santo, and L.M. Nunes. "Impact of a Strategy to Prevent the Introduction of Non-Breast Milk and Complementary Foods during the First Six Months of Life: A Randomized Clinical Trial with Adolescent Mothers and Grandmothers. *Early Human Development* 88 (2012): 357–361.

- Grandmothers to Grandmothers Campaign of the Stephen Lewis Foundation: http://www.grandmotherscampaign.org/

- Grandparent relationship: Geurts, T., T. van Tilburg, and A-R. Poortman. "The Grandparent–Grandchild Relationship in Childhood and Adulthood: A Matter of Continuation?" *Personal Relationships.* 19 (2012): 267–278.

- Grandparent rights: http://www.canadianelderlaw. ca/Grandparents%20Access%20Law.htm http://www. grandparentsrights.org

- Grandparents: "Across the Generations: Grandparents and Grandchildren." 2003. Statistics Canada, Catalogue No. 11–008 7, http://www.bccf.ca/all/resources/quick-facts-grandparenting.

- Grief: http://grief.com/the-five-stages-of-grief

- Gripe water: http://jrs.sagepub.com/content/93/4/172.citation

- Hearing: http://www.cdc.gov/ncbddd/hearingloss/facts.html

- Hip Dysplasia: http://www.hipdysplasia.org/developmental-dysplasia-of-the-hip/hip-healthy-swaddling/

- Infection: http://www.ncbi.nlm.nih.gov/pubmedhealth/PMH0002342/

- Intense parenting: Rizzo, K.M., H.H. Schiffrin, and M. Liss. "Insight into the Parenthood Paradox: Mental Health Outcomes of Intensive Mothering." *Journal of Child and Family Studies.* (2012). DOI 10.1007/s10826-012-9615-z.

- It take a village: http://www.janecowenfletcher.com/books/

- IVF: http://www.ivf.ca/results.htm

- Jaundice: http://www.cps.ca/documents/position/hyperbilirubinemia-newborn

- Lactation consultants: http://www.iblce.org

- Mattress monitors: http://www.toysrus.com/product/index.jsp?productId=2970307

- Midwives association: http://www.canadianmidwives.org

- Mindfulness: http://www.mindfulnessmeditationcentre.org/stress.htm

- Multigenerational family: Bengston, V. "Beyond the Nuclear Family: The Increasing Importance of Multigenerational Bonds." *Journal of Marriage and Family.* 63, 1, 1–16, 2001 DOI: 10.1111/j.1741-3737.2001.00001.x

- Nap Nanny: http://www.huffingtonpost.com/2012/12/27/ nap-nanny-recall_n_2369226.html.Newborn Screening: http://www.cdc.gov/ncbddd/pediatricgenetics/newborn_screening. html

- Pacifiers: http://www.pediatricsdigest.mobi/content/116/5/e716.full, http://www.cps.ca/english/statements/cp/cp03-01.htm

- Pregnancy: "The Sensible Guide to a Healthy Pregnancy," www. phac-aspc.gc.ca/hp-gs/pdf/hpguide-eng.pdf

- Private detailed ultrasound: http://www.uc-baby.com/en/index.php

- Registered Education Savings Plan: http://www.cra-arc.gc.ca/tx/ ndvdls/tpcs/resp-reee/menu-eng.html?=slnk http://www.hrsdc.gc.ca/ eng/learning/education_savings/public/resp.shtml

- Religion (Archie Bunker baptizes baby Joey): http://www.youtube. com/watch?v=D1cp9hZwWZA

- Safety: http://www.healthycanadians.gc.ca/kids-enfants/index-eng.php

- Sarah Blaffer Hardy. *Mother Nature: A History of Mothers, Infants, and Natural Selection*. New York: Pantheon Books, 1999.

- SIDS: http://www.cidc.gov.sids/ http://www.familypracticenews. com/news/more-top-news/single-view/aap-s-new-sids-stoppers-cleared-cribs-no-cosleeping/a7e304621a.html

- Skin care: http://www.caringforkids.cps.ca/handouts/skin_care_for_ your_baby

- Skype: http://www.skype.com/intl/en-us/home

- Safe sleep: http://www.cps.ca/english/statements/cp/cp04-02.htm http://www.phac-aspc.gc.ca/hp-ps/dca-dea/stages-etapes/childhood-enfance_0-2/sids/ssb_brochure-eng.php

- Sleep sacs: https://www.halosleep.com/

- Sleep (Dana Oberman): http://www.youtube.com/watch?v=CWvvlu3-VE4&feature=related

- Solids: http://www.healthychildren.org/English/ages-stages/baby/feeding-nutrition/Pages/Switching-To-Solid-Foods.aspx?nfstatus=401&nftoken=00000000-0000-0000-0000-000000000000&nfstatusdescription=ERROR%3a+No+local+token

- http://www.hc-sc.gc.ca/fn-an/nutrition/infant-nourisson/recom/index-eng.php#a7

- http://www.cdc.gov/nutrition/everyone/basics/vitamins/iron.html

- Smoking: http://www.lung.ca/protect-protegez/tobacco-tabagisme/second-secondaire/thirdhand-tertiaire_e.php

- Sunscreen: http://www.hc-sc.gc.ca/hl-vs/pubs/sun-sol/babies_child-bebes_enfant-eng.php

- Swaddling: http://www.youtube.com/watch?v=PnJ7ykXDpDA

- Teething necklaces: http://www.hc-sc.gc.ca/cps-spc/child-enfant/equip/necklaces-colliers-eng.php

- Tiger Mom: http://amychua.com/

- Toy ratings and safety, US: http://www.cpsc.gov/

- Toy ratings and safety, Canada: http://www.hc-sc.gc.ca/cps-spc/pubs/cons/toy_safe-jouet_secur-eng.php

- Umbilical cord: http://www.healthychildren.org/English/ages-stages/baby/bathing-skin-care/Pages/Umbilical-Cord-Care.aspx?nfstatus=401&nftoken=00000000-0000-0000-0000-000000000000&nfstatusdescription=ERROR%3a+No+local+token

- Vision: http://kidshealth.org/parent/general/eyes/vision.html#

- Vitamin D in breastfed babies: http://www.hc-sc.gc.ca/fn-an/nutrition/infant-nourisson/vita_d_qa-qr-eng.php

ABBREVIATIONS

AAP—American Academy of Pediatrics

ACOG—American Congress of Obstetricians and Gynecologists

AED—Automated External Defibrillator

AKA—Also known as

AP—Attachment parenting

ARM—Artificial rupture of the membranes

ART—Assisted reproductive technology

BLW—Baby-led weaning

BMI—Body mass index

BPA—Bisphenol A

BPM—Beats per minute

BPP—Biophysical profile

CDC—Centers for Disease Control and Prevention

CIO—Crying it out

CPR—Cardiopulmonary resuscitation

DiL—Daughter-in-law

EBM—Expressed breast milk

GBS—Group B streptococcal septicemia

IV—Intravenous

LC—Lactation consultant

MiL—Mother-in-law

NVP—Nausea and vomiting in pregnancy

SBS—Shaken baby syndrome

SIDS—Sudden infant death syndrome

SOGC—Society of Obstetricians and Gynecologists of Canada

SoL—Signs of labor

SRM—Spontaneous rupture of the membranes

TOLAC—Trial of labor after Cesarean section

U/S—Ultrasound

VBAC—Vaginal birth after Cesarean section

WHO—World Health Organization

INDEX

Abbreviations, 203
Adoption
    Baby, 182
    Grandmother, 182
Allergies
    Breastfeeding, 100, 110-111
    Prevention, 110
    Solids, 106-107
Anomalies, 55-56, 183, 192
Anxiety
    Mother, 20-21, 24
    See also separation anxiety,
    stranger anxiety
Assisted reproduction
    Artificial insemination, 53
    Egg donation, 53
    In vitro fertilization, 53
    Surrogacy, 52-53
Attachment parenting   .
    7 B's, 172-173
    Guilt, 173
    In practice, 162, 173

Baby sign language, 174
Babysitting, 37-40
    Holiday sitting, 40
    Nannies and Childminders, 40
    Their house or yours, 38-40
Baby Wearing, 114, 165-166, 172
Bathing, 94-96
Birth
    See Labor and birth
Behavior
    Crying it out/CIO, 140-
    141, 173
    Discipline, 176-178
    Meltdown, 176
    Separation anxiety, 175-176
    Stranger anxiety, 175-176
    Terrible twos, 176
Bottlefeeding
    Artificial baby milk, 101-103
    Bottles, 103-104
    Formula, 102-103
    Heating, 103-104

Boundaries
    Babysitting, 38
    Sandwich generation, 27
    Clubhouse, 27
    Breastfeeding, 98-101, 109,
    110, 111, 113-114, , 116, 118-
    119, 134, 172, 193, 194
    Exclusive Breastfeeding, 98-99
    Expressed Breast Milk
    (EBM), 98
    Hooter hiders, 101
    How long?, 99-100
    If you didn't breastfeed..., 98
    Iron, 99
    Lactation consultant, 68-69
    On demand, 98
    Pumping, 98
    Storing, 98-99
    Support, 100-101
    Vitamin D, 99, 106

Care providers
    Doula, 68-69, 74, 100
    Family Dr., 68
    Lactation consultant, 68,
    100, 200
    Midwife, 68, 196
    Nurse, 68
    Obstetrician, 68, 195-196
Challenges – see communication,
    emotions,
    parenting
    Adoption, 182
    Anomalies/disabilities, 55,
    183, 197
    Death, 184

Dislike babies, 188
    Distance, 179-180
    Divorce, 181-182
    Feeling unappreciated,
    188-189
    Grief, 185-187
    Miscarriage, 184
    Multiples, 54-55
    Single-parent, 180-181
Circumcision, 115-116
    Girls, 116
Clothing
    Blankets, 134, 139, 142,
    163, 165
    Diapers, 118-123
    Sleep sacs, 139, 201
    Onsies, 167
    Quilts, 134, 163
Colic
    Causes, 113
    Cures, 113-115, 166
    Gripe water, 114
    Probiotics, 114
Common baby issues
    Colic and gas, 113-115
    Cradle cap, 112-113
Communication
    Advice, 33-35
    Baby sign language, 174
    Daughter-in-law, 43-45
    Discipline, 37, 47, 171, 176-178
    History, 18-19
    How not to alienate the par-
    ents, 35-36
    Other grandparents, 46-47
    Right – fighter, 32-33

Son, 45-46
Son-in-law, 45-46
Step grandmother, 47-48
Cord-See Umbilical cord
CPR, 154-156
    Back blows, 153
    Choking, 107, 109, 117, 118, 151-155
    Courses, 155-156
    Gagging, 151
Cradle cap, 112-113
    Causes, 112
    Coconut and olive oil, 113
    Cures, 112-113
Crib
    Bumper pads, 134, 142
    Death – see SIDS
    Sleeping, 134, 138, 142
Culture, 10-11, 88, 115-116, 137, 172

Death, 98, 127, 130, 133-134, 142, 147, 150,157,170, 184, 186 – see SIDS, grief
    Baby, 184
    Grief – parents, 185-187
    Grief – you, 187
Delivery – see labor and birth
Depression – see emotions
Diapers – see potty training
    Baby powder, 124
    Bag, 124, 125, 166
    Cloth, 119-121, 122
    Creams, 122-123
    Diaper free, 119
    Diapering systems, 120-121

Disposables, 121-122
Disposing, 121-122
Elimination communication, 119
Rash, 122-123
Swimmers, 121, 122
Washing, 121
Wipes, 124
Discipline, 171, 176-178
Distance, 179-180
    Skype etc., 179
Divorce – see In-laws
    Boomerang kids, 180-181
    Rights, 181-182

Emotions—see postpartum
    Anxiety, 20-21
    Blues, 20
    Communication, 31
    Depression: antenatal & postpartum, 21-23
    How to help, 24-25
    History, 18-19
    Pinks, 19-20
    Perinatal mood disorders, 19
    Positive mental health, 29-30
    Psychosis, 23
    Support, 26
    Taking care of you, 26-27
Equipment
    Baby wearing, 165-166
    Bumbo, 160-161
    Car seats, 157-159
    Clothing, 166-167
    Diaper bag, 166
    Gates, 162

High chairs,160
Playpen/play yard, 161-162
Safety, 144-145, 169-170
Strollers, 159
Toys, 167-170
Walkers, 159-160

Feeding – see allergies,
    bottlefeeding,
    breastfeeding, solids
    Baby-led weaning, 109, 197
    Beverages, liquids, 111-112
    Prepared foods, 110
    Gluten sensitivity/celiac dis-
    ease, 111
    Readiness to eat, 106
    Solids, 105
    Toddler, 108-109
Flathead – see Plagiocephaly
Financial
    Insurance, 50, 69
    Savings plans, 49-50

Grief – see death
    Parents, 185-187
    You, 187
Grandmother
    Benefits, 1-3
    Hypothesis, 4
    Investment, 3-4
    Memories, 4-5

High chair– see equipment

Immunizations
    Autism, 130

Baby, 130-131
Flu, 63-64
Pertussis, 130-131
Infant – see Skin-to-skin, umbili-
cal cord,
    jaundice, nutrition
    Bath time, 94-96
    Early care, 93-94
    Eyes, 96-97, 116,128-129, 133
    Hearing, 128
    Tests and screens, 55-57
    Vitamin K, 96-97
Infections – see immunizations
    GBS, 62-63, 203
    Wash hands, 63
    Reduce risk, 63
In-laws – see communication, cul-
ture, relationships, religion,
son-in-law, daughter-in-law

Jaundice
    Bilirubin, 97, 116-117
    Kernicterus, 116-117
    Treatment, 117

Labor and birth – see placenta
    Activity, 78
    Being there, 73-74
    Castor oil, 69, 77
    C – section, 83
    Enemas, 80
    Episiotomy/tears, 82-83
    Epidural/spinal, 84-85
    Forceps, 82
    Herbal remedies, 78
    Home birth, 74

Induction of birth, 75-78
Intravenous, 79
Laughing gas, 85
Lotus birth, 86
Membranes rupture, 72, 76
Monitors, 79
Nipple stimulation, 77
Nutrition, 80
Pain relief, 84
Placenta, 79, 83, 86
Preterm, 54, 62, 79, 95, 97, 128, 129, 137,
Process, 71-73
Pushing, 80-81
Ripening of cervix, 75
Safety, 75
Sexual intercourse, 76-77
Shaving, 80
Spinal, 83, 84-85
Stripping/sweeping the membranes, 75-76
TOLAC, 83-84
Vacuum, 81
VBAC, 83-84
Water birth, 74-75
Your role, 73-74
Limitations
Clubhouse, 27
Health, 14-15
Hearing, 15
Physical, 14-15
Time, 26-29
Vision, 15
Lotus birth, 86

Milestones, 106, 131-133
Money-See Financial
Monitors
Apnea, 137
Baby, 136-137, 139
Fetal, 79

Names
Baby, 9-10
Grandmother, 8-9
Nausea and vomiting, 51, 57-58, 192
Newborn – see infant

Pacifiers, soothers, binkies, 45, 103, 104-105, 117, 201
Parenting, 5-6, 12-14, 34, 36, 141, 162, 171-173, 191
Attachment, 36, 138, 141, 161, 172-173, 193
Helicopter parenting, 172
Intense parenting, 22
Over parenting, 172
Sleep, 137-139
Tiger, 171-172
Perfect, 6-7
Placenta, 79, 83, 86
Eating, 86
Nonseverance, 86
Placentaphagia, 86
Plagiocephaly, 135-136
Flathead, 135
Reducing risk, 135-136
Back to sleep, 134
SIDS, 34, 98, 104, 105, 133-134, 137-

139, 142, 148,
Tummy time, 143, 163
Play
    Playpen/play yard, 161-162
    Toys, 167-169
    You, 169
Postpartum, 87-92 – see also
    emotions
    Changes, 87
    Coming home, 88-89
    Emotions, 89
    Flow, Hemorrhage, 89-90
    How to help, 24-25, 90-92
    Hospital stay, 87-88
    Housework, 82-83, 90-92
    Support, 26, 88
    Visiting, 42-43, 88
    When to come, 89
Potty Training, 119, 125
    Elimination communication,
    119
    Potties, 125
    Timing, 125
    Three day method, 125
Poisons – see safety
Pregnancy
    Assisted reproduction, 52
    Conception, 52-53
    Flu, 63-64
    Folic acid (Folate), 57, 58-59
    Infections, 62-63
    Movement of baby, 64-65, 75
    Multiples, 54-55
    Nausea and vomiting, 51, 57-
    58, 192
    Obesity, 60, 62

Tests, 55-57
Ultrasound, 55-57, 65, 66,
    79, 183
Vitamins, 57, 58-59
Weight, 59-62
Worry – baby, 64-66
Worry – mother, 66
Prenatal classes, 12, 67, 100
Psychosis—see emotions

Religion, 10, 201
Relationships – see communica-
    tion, discipline, emotions,
    Clubhouse, 27
    Coping, 29
    Parent first, 36-37
    Taking care of you, 26-27
    Visiting, 42-43
Resources, 191-196
    American Academy of Pediat-
    rics, 195
    American College of
    Nurse-Midwives, 196
    American Congress of Obste-
    tricians and Gynecologists, 196
    Attachment Parenting Inter-
    national, 193
    Babycenter, 67, 132, 193
    Bibliography, 197-203
    Canadian Pediatric Society,
    115, 195
    Care providers, 68-69
    Commercial, 193-194
    Consumer Reports, 194
    Dr. Sears, 13, 36, 114, 141, 194
    Government agencies, 194-195

Information overload, 66

Kellymom, 100, 194

La Leche League, 100, 141, 193

March of Dimes, 192

Motherisk, 58, 114, 192

Online, websites, 67, 192-196

Penny Simkin, 84, 194

Postpartum Support International, 193

Prenatal classes, 67

Private organizations, 192-193

Professional, 191, 195-196

Social media, 67

Society of Obstetricians and Gynecologists of Canada, 196

Role model, 11-12

Routines, 37, 39, 40, 141

Rules, 73, 142, 173, 176-177, 181

Safety – see CPR, smoking

Batteries, 147

Car seats, 157-159

Choking, 107, 109, 117-118, 151-156

CPR, 154-156

Detergent pods, 147

Door latches, 144-145, 147

Gagging, 151-152

Gates, 162

Insect repellent, 150-151

Magnets, 147

Medications, 146

Pets, 146

Playpens/play yards, 161-162

Sleep – see Sleep

Smoking, 134, 148-149

Sun, 149-150

Walkers, 159-160

Water, 145

Your house, 144, 169-170

Separation anxiety, 175-176

Shaken Baby Syndrome, 133

Siblings

Toddler regression, 41

Helping, 41-42

SIDS, 133-134

Causes, 133-134

Reduce risk, 134

Single parent, 180-181

Skin

Cradle cap, 112-113

Jaundice, 116-117

Rashes & irritation, 122-124, 129

Skin-to-skin, 94

Sleep– see also SIDS

Baby, 133-134

Back lying, 134

Bed sharing, 137-139

Co-sleeping, 137-139

Crib, 133, 134, 138, 142

Crying it out (CIO), 140-141, 173

Dr. Karp, 13, 194

Flathead, 135-136

Mother, 19, 20, 23, 86, 88

Position, 34, 134

Sleep sac, 139

Sleep training, 139-140

Sleep routine, 141

Surfaces, 142

Tummy time, 143

Smoking
  Secondhand, 148
  Thirdhand, 148
Solids, 105
  Allergies, 110-111
  Baby-led weaning, 109
  Choking, 107, 109
  Choices, 106-108
  Gagging/gag reflex, 151-152
  Hot dogs, 152
  Hummus, 108
  Introduction of solids,
  107-108
  Obesity, 108
  Organic, 110
  Popcorn, 107, 152
Son
  Depression, 25
  Role, 45-46
  Sleep, 46
  Son-in-law, 45-46
Soothers – Pacifiers, 45, 103, 104-
  105, 117, 201
Stranger anxiety, 175-176
Strollers
  Chariot-style, 159
  Travel systems, 159
Sudden Infant Death Syn-
  drome-see SIDS
Sun, sunburn, 149-150
  Baby, 149-150
  Hat, 150
  Glasses, 150
  Sunscreen, 149-150

Swaddling
  To swaddle or not? 164-165
  Receiving blankets, 165

Teething, 117
  Comfort, 117
  Necklaces, 118
Toilet training – see potty
  training
Toys, 163, 167-170
  Ages, 168
  Safety, 169-170
  Your house, 169-170
Traditions, 5, 7-8
  Keepsakes, 8
Tummy time – see also SIDS,
  sleep
  How, 143
  When?, 143
  Why?, 143
  How long?, 143

Umbilical cord, 76, 95, 96, 127, 202
  Drying, 96
  Non-severance, 86

Vaccinations – see immunizations
Visiting, 42-43, 88
Vitamins – see also pregnancy
  Baby, 101, 146
  Folic acid, 57, 58-59
  Mother, 57, 58-59
  Vitamin A, 58
  Vitamin D, 58, 99

Walkers, 159-160
    Stationary, 160-161
Water birth, 74-75
Websites – see Resources

You
    Go forth gently, 189-190
    Taking care of you, 26-27
    What if you don't like it?,
    188-189

About the Author

Angela Bowen, RN PhD is a Registered Nurse and Associate Professor in the College of Nursing and Department of Psychiatry at the University of Saskatchewan. She has almost forty years of experience caring for pregnant women and new mothers, or teaching others the best ways to care for them. Angela researches maternal mental health, and knows the importance of a grandmother's support for a new mother.

As a new grandmother, she felt prepared for the role, but discovered that much had changed since she had children. Now, she is an active and involved grandparent with her young grandsons, often giving advice to others on how to succeed as a grandparent, from the most up-to-date facts on pregnancy, labor and birth, infant nutrition and sleep, attachment parenting, equipment, and child safety, to improving family relationships with the new mother and her partner.